THE GHETTO AND THE UNDERCLASS

Research in Ethnic Relations Series

The New Helots
Migrants in the International Division of Labour
Robin Cohen

Black Radicalism and the Politics of De-industrialisation
The Hidden History of Indian Foundry Workers
Mark Duffield

The Ghetto and the Underclass
Essays on Race and Social Policy
John Rex

The Ghetto and the Underclass
Essays on Race and Social Policy

JOHN REX

Research Professor in Ethnic Relations
University of Warwick

Avebury
Aldershot · Brookfield USA · Hong Kong · Singapore · Sydney

Published by
Avebury
Gower Publishing Company Limited
Gower House, Croft Road, Aldershot, Hants GU11 3HR,
England

Gower Publishing Company
Old Post Road, Brookfield, Vermont 05036,
United States of America.

British Library Cataloguing in Publication Data

Rex, John, *1925*
    The ghetto and the underclass: essays on race and social policy. — (Research in ethnic relations).
    1. Great Britain. Race relations.
    I. Title.   II. Series.
    305.8′00941

Library of Congress Cataloging-in-Publication Data

Rex, John
    The ghetto and the underclass: essays on race and social policy/by John Rex.
        p.   cm. — (Research in ethnic relations series)
    Bibliography: p.
    Includes index.
    1. Urban poor — Great Britain — Social conditions. 2. Great Britain — Race relations.
    3. Great Britain — Ethnic relations. 4. Great Britain — Social policy. 5. Urban policy — Great Britain.
    I. Title.   II. Series.
    HV4085.A5R49 1988
    305.8′00941 — dc19   88–1276
                                                                                        CIP

ISBN 0 566 05651 8

Printed and bound in Great Britain by
Biddles Limited, Guildford and King's Lynn

Contents

Introduction

The aim of this book is to offer a critical perspective on the way in which the relations between British society and its South Asian and Caribbean minorities have developed over a twenty-five year period. Most of the chapters are rewritten versions of polemical papers given on particular issues during that time. Although they are contextually situated, taken together they serve to illustrate a general theme. This is not merely that there is a danger of 'racism' in British society, but that the proposed remedies for this 'racism' are themselves confused and therefore damaging to Asian and Black people. The result is that the perspective offered is far from a popular one. It challenges many of the vested interests in the 'race relations industry', in social administration and what passes for social science itself.

Most of these essays were written between 1979 and 1986 and in some ways the surrounding circumstances have changed. Specifically Conservative policy under Mrs Thatcher has taken on a more clearly ideological form and many of the assumptions in the essays about a received wisdom of a Fabian kind are less true than they were. Moreover, since much of the kind of change advocated here assumes action by local as well as central government, the undermining of local government power envisaged by the third Thatcher government, must make change at that level less relevant. In the case of the schools for example, if the carrying out of a multi-cultural and anti-racial education had come to depend on local authority initiative, such initiatives are likely to be seriously undermined by the proposal that schools should be able to opt out of local authority control. Again the decline of Council housing means that the issue of racial discrimination must now be faced more in the owner-occupier and privately rented sector than on the Council estates. All of the policy issues discussed here, moreover, have to be seen against a background of three million unemployed.

Despite all this, however, the issues raised here are still important. Racial discrimination and segregation are not to be attributed solely to Thatcherism. It is important to understand that even if there were a change of central government policy in a more socialist or welfarist direction, the problem of racial discrimination and segregation would still remain and specific new policies would have to be developed to arrest the development of the ghetto and the creation of a Black underclass.

The earlier essays contained here deal with a period of racist panic in which, faced with the relatively sudden arrival of Black and Asian immigrants, British society at all levels threw up barriers of discrimination to prevent these immigrants from competing for scarce resources. What is much less widely recognised is that such discrimination was not merely a function of free market decisions. It was also characteristic of bureaucratic socialist institutions set up to achieve justice for the native British working class. In my work with Robert Moore in Sparkbrook I had shown that Blacks and Asians were discriminated against in the public housing sector just as much or more than they were in the free market. The working class through the Labour Party had developed the council housing system to ensure housing rights for its own members. It now used what Parkin (1979) calls 'usurpatory closure' to deny the rights which it had won to newcomers.

It was by no means easy to get a hearing if one campaigned against discrimination in the allocation of council houses. Most social reformers worked through the Labour Party and it was often the Labour Party which managed the system of housing discrimination. The same was true of much social science, influenced as it was by ideas derived from campaigns of social reform in the 1930s. Whether Fabian or Marxist, it had little space for recognising that the interests of the British working class as understood by them at least were or could be in conflict with those of any other group.

Campaigning against racial discrimination, i.e. trying to ensure that racial and ethnic minorities had equal rights or 'life-chances', was in any case difficult because it was not always easy to prove that a particular individual 'gate-keeper' was responsible for specific acts of discrimination. I was therefore inclined to argue that the concrete evidence of disadvantage should be taken as evidence of such discrimination. A quite different doctrine however came to occupy the field. This was that there might not be any such thing as discrimination at all and that the sole problem was one of largely accidental disadvantage. Thus when I was looking to the government to intervene to alter council house allocation schemes which were discriminatory, I was told that the problem was not one of discrimination at all but simply that there were large areas in which housing, as such, regardless of its occupants, was in a bad state. Far easier, it seemed, to deal with an environmental problem than one which involved human responsibility.

In the late nineteen sixties nearly all policy discussion was devoted to environmental questions and questions of disadvantage leaving out any consideration of questions of racial discrimination. Thus no attention was given to the question of ghetto-formation as such, only to that of how physical conditions in the 'inner-cities' could be improved. By then Blacks and Asians were already concentrated in the next-worse houses after slum-clearance (had they been in the 'slums' they would have been eligible for rehousing) and it was decided that these houses should be 'improved' rather than replaced. There was to be no new slum-clearance programme and the next-worst houses were to be used to house immigrant families in the stage of family-completion. Instead of being moved to council houses the Blacks and Asians were offered council mortgages or Housing Association tenancies in the improvement areas. They were not to be denied housing, only offered an alternative type of housing. This was a recipe for segregation and ghettoisation.

Meanwhile the deprivations which the racial minorities suffered were systematically treated as problems of generalised disadvantage. Priority areas were established in education, an Urban programme was instituted to deal with the problems of the disadvantaged poor and Commuinity Development programmes were begun with the aim of discovering the new needs of the Inner City and providing for them. All of these programmes systematically avoided consideration of whether racial discrimination ensured that Black and Asian minorities were more likely to suffer disadvantage.

This last point was made a matter of principle in the White Paper, Policy for the Inner Cities (Department of the Environment 1977a). Specifically it suggested that racial discrimination was not its problem and that this was a matter for the Commission for Racial Equality. Still worse, however, as I show in several of the chapters which follow, when aid was advocated for the Inner City it was coupled with the notion of population replacement carried out in the name of 'dispersal and balance'. Blacks and Asians, at first forced to live in the Inner City by segregation processes, were now to be encouraged to disperse. Improvement of the Inner City was to mean, inter-alia, getting rid of their Black population. It is perhaps fortunate that lack of resources prevented this policy from being systematically carried out.

Social policy thus developed without any serious consideration of problems of racial discrimination. This was held to be the province of the Commission for Racial Equality which succeeded the Community Relations Commission and the Race Relations Board in 1976. It remains to consider what the achievements of this body have been.

One fundamental difficulty which the new commission faced was that it was required both to work for enforcement of minority rights and to do promotional work to persuade the White majority into a more friendly stance. This is a fundamental difficulty and one which requires all the political skill of the Chairman and his Commissioners to deal with. Inevitably however it has tended to give to the Commission pronouncements the quality of the moral reproofs of a maiden aunt and the Commission is hardly taken seriously by the media and the general public. Coupled with the lack of adequate resources to carry out its enforcement task, the Commission by itself has been a very weak force indeed for countering racial discrimination despite the fact that the 1976 Act is in many ways a very strong act allowing for an attack on indirect as well as direct discrimination.

One point in the 1976 Act was of particular importance. This was Section 71 which called upon, even though it did not require, Local Authorities to take action to promote equality of opportunity. At first this produced little response, but after the urban disturbances of 1981 numerous district as well as metropolitan councils set up equal opportunity and race relations committees and departments. What is perjoratively called the 'race relations industry' has therefore grown enormously in terms of the number of jobs created for race relations and equal opportunity officers.

The existence of these many posts in local government undoubtedly has some educative effect. It symbolises the fact that there is an official commitment to racial equality and it gives legitimacy to numerous initiatives, which twenty years ago would have been considered entirely illegitimate and outside the scope of local government. Nonetheless it is necessary to question whether these various departments are actually achieving much by way of promoting racial equality. It has been said cynically in the United States that the main effect of Poverty Programmes has been to ease the poverty of the poverty workers and it might well be asked in Britain whether the plethora of committees and departments concerned with race relations has done anything more than to create a new artificially sponsored middle class in the Black and Asian community. A point may well arise at which the definition of their jobs becomes more important for those concerned than the promotion of equality of opportunity amongst the mass of the minority population or actually appears to them as a sufficient sign of the attainment of that equality of opportunity.

A clear commitment to the goal of equality of oportunity is nonetheless significant in the fight against racial discrimination. What are more questionable are policies within which this goal becomes blurred or confused with other possibly contradictory goals. This is the case, for example, where multi-cultural policies are advocated as a means of implementing equality of opportunity. Multi-culturalism may be important in its own right. Other things being equal there may well be an important case for respecting the different cultural practices of ethnic minorities. Doing so could actually help to control racism. It is also the case, however, that multi-cultural educational and other policies might be adopted in order to offer minorities an alternative education which is different and inferior. Thus one tends to find an unholy alliance between those who are only concerned to provide different and inferior services to minorities and those from the minorities as well as from the majority community who can make a living out of the maintenance of inferiority, which nevertheless professes what sounds like a noble and even egalitarian ideal of multi-culturalism. It is here that what is called 'the race relations industry' flourishes.

One particular means within this industry both in the schools and more widely in the professions and in the government is provided by what is called 'racial awareness training'. Resting upon a somewhat idealistic theory that racism is the product of unconscious attitudes which can be eliminated by bringing them to consciousness, this type of programme has been widely used in the United States. Insofar as it is coupled with a clear government commitment to racial equality it is possible that such programmes may have some signifiance in deracialising a society and countering discrimination. What is far more questionable is the use of such programmes on their own where the commitment to racial equality of those in power is non-existent or ambiguous. This is often the case in Britain where racial awareness training programmes are adopted. At worst they flourish because as one commentator (Bhagat 1986) suggests a few blacks can make money out of guilty whites.

The existence of a race-relations industry, largely staffed by minority members, is a very real fact in Britain today and is strengthened by the process of implementation of Section 71 of the Race Relations Act. It is difficult to criticise because by no means all of those who occupy such posts are charlatans and opportunists. There is a case for equality of opportunity officers; there is a case for multi-culturalism; and there is a case for education against racism. But each of these policies has its own pathology and the existence of such pathological variants must be pointed out before we hail the development of equality of opportunity and multi-cultural policies as a sign of the disappearance of racism.

One natural check on the development of opportunism in this area is provided by the political actions of minority people themselves. Gradually this is taking the form of political representation in local councils and it may soon be evident in national parliamentary elections. Alternatively it may take the form of violent extra-parliamentary action against the police. Black political action in both of these forms has been evident in Britain in the eighties. Opportunists and careerists will no doubt use such actions to advance their own interests but they are far more subject to control in those circumstances than when they staff paternalistically provided programmes. The position adopted in these essays is

4

that it is ultimately through political action by the minority rank and file, and only through this, that racial discrimination and racism will be defeated.

Crucial in this fight against racism is the question of police accountability. The British police have been shown to be thoroughly infected with racism and enquiries into the riots of 1981 and 1985 have shown them as bringing archaic colonialist attitudes to bear on policing inner city areas. At the same time the police have powerful support in the media and it is difficult to make public criticism of their behaviour without being denounced as some kind of anarchist or terrorist. A measure of the situation is provided by the fact that the Scarman proposals for reform which are minimal and moderate are generally thought of as the extreme of radicalism. These issues are discussed in the final chapters of this book.

Running through this discussion of the riots and other political activity is the question of how far the struggles of ethnic minorities for just treatment merge with those of the struggles of the native working class, the disadvantaged and the unemployed. The position taken here is that the minorities cannot rely solely on working-class political action. Inevitably in times of recession their actions merge with those of the disadvantaged and the unemployed, but structurally, because of the fact of racial discrimination, they have their own class-like position in society and that position must be fought for in its own right even if sometimes it will have to be fought for within a wider working-class struggle. There is a danger that both Fabianism and Marxism will be offered in reductionist versions as explanations of race and ethnic relations and these essays must be seen as a corrective to both of these tendencies.

Most of the essays contained here are published for the first time. Chapter One is based on an address to the European Academy in London in 1982. Chapter Two is a version of an address to the Social Administration Association in 1983. Chapter Three is the substance of my James Seth Memorial Lecture in Edinburgh in 1983. Race, Law and Politics was an address to the British Sociological Association in 1979. Chapter Five is based upon the John Madge Memorial Lecture in 1982. Chapter Seven is a working paper in connection with my research in Handsworth. Chapter Nine is a paper given to a conference on the Swann Report in Sunderland in 1986.

Chapter Six on Race and the Urban System was first published in a book entitled Urbanism and Urbanisation edited by Noel Iverson and published by E.J. Brill. Chapter Eight was published in Multi-Cultural Education edited by Modgil, Verma, Mallick and Modgil published by the Falmer Press. Chapter Ten appeared in the International Journal of Urban and Regional Research Vol. 6, No.1. Chapter Eleven appeared in Law and Order in British Politics edited by Phillip Norton and published by Gower. I am grateful to those concerned for permitting the republication of these pieces.

I New priorities in social policy

In recent years social policy in many countries has centred around a new focus. In the immediate post-war period the focus was on the maintenance of full employment, the provision of social insurance in times of transitional unemployment and the development of a variety of forms of social provision in such areas as education, health, and more personal and family problems. In Britain the two central volumes around which a philosophy of social administration was evolved were the Beveridge Report (Beveridge 1942) and Beveridge's book, Full Employment in a Free Society (Beveridge 1944). In the years of prosperity in the sixties and those of recession which followed in the seventies, however, it seemed clear that, however important the basic structure which the philosophy of Beveridge had provided, the advanced industrial societies were beset by and riven by wholly new problems and divisions. Gaps opened up between the secure and stably employed and the New Poor, existing social services were seen as insenitive to a wide range of new needs, Inner City areas were abandoned in a process of residential and industrial suburbanisation, recession, when it came, hit hardest at the new Inner City poor, the urban population was joined by substantial minorities of immigrants from poorer and sometimes former colonial countries, racism emerged as a problem, and in some countries the Inner City exploded in violence which was seen to be amplified rather than controlled by insensitive policing. It is this set of problems which is commonly referred to in Britain and the United States at least as The Problem of the Inner City.

In the development of social policy for the eighties and nineties it is useful to begin with this definition of the problem as an Inner City problem, because that is how the terms of the debate are set politically. In doing so, however, it is essential that we distinguish the various components of this problem and show how it is too often misdiagnosed as a result of simplistic labelling and the irrelevant application of outworn ideologies.

The problem of the Inner City, or sometimes, more generally, the problem of the cities, moved to the centre of politics in the United States during the Kennedy, Johnson and the early stages of the Nixon administrations, and almost equalled the Vietnam war as a political issue, when, following the Watts riots of 1966, there was widespread rioting in a large number of cities in the Long Hot Summer of

1967. In a society not well disposed to welfare measures which might be seen to interfere with private economic enterprise a whole range of new initiatives were developed to lay the basis of a new social policy.

The oldest theme in this new policy was that which concerned the process of urbanisation and suburbanisation itself. From a situation in which the great cities had been seen as the very centres of high civilisation and culture, the United States has moved to a situation in which these cities were seen as desolate, deserted and dangerous places. There seemed to be a secular change occurring within this civilisation in which the natural process of urban development was producing a wholly new ideal style of life and the 'Inner City' remained as a festering sore on the body politic. The problem was to treat that sore, to provide relative health to the Inner City, and to ensure that its eruption did not destroy the whole of urban civilisation itself. However much the society might be committed to private enterprise and self-help, public assistance had to be given to the people of the Inner City in terms of poverty programmes and other forms of assistance.

The nature of American society was such, however, that the new Inner City conflicts inevitably had a racial dimension. The evolution of that society was one in which neither the Deep South, whose institutions had developed around the slave plantation using Black slaves, nor the urban ghettoes of the North to which the surplus population from the South migrated, had yet been fully incorporated into a democratic capitalist society. Immigrants from Europe had arrived in wave after wave in the hundred years after the Civil War and they had found their way into the social and political system, and, indeed more than that, to making and controlling that system, but the Blacks of the South and the ghettoes had yet to realise in social terms the rights to which they seemed entitled under the constitution. A long process of struggle to win these rights had begun to produce results by the fifties and, inevitably, when any other basis of conflict emerged in the society, it overlapped with the struggle for Black rights. The urban riots of 1967 were Black riots because amongst those losing out in economic competition or left behind in the Inner City, the majority were Black.

The social policies developed in the United States, therefore, centred, not simply on poverty programmes, but upon the notion of Affirmative Action. Because ordinary anti-discrimination measures did not seem to have ensured equal social participation by Black Americans a new notion of Positive Discrimination emerged. The rules of free and open competition or rewards had to be altered to ensure that some Blacks at least could advance in education, in economic opportunity, and in preferment for prestigious government employment. Unlikely though such developments might have been, given the legacy of White superiority and the ideology of free competition, there now seemed to be a political imperative to promote at least some Blacks and to integrate the nation.

The urban problem facing America also faced the nations of Europe. There too the suburban trend was beginning to produce a desolate inner city urban desert. True, the trend towards suburbanisation was probably stronger in Britain than in continental countries and the process was likely to be regulated by public intervention more than in the United States, but something of the same pattern was to be seen in some degree in all countries. The cities were increasingly poor both in terms of their fiscal base and in terms of the standard of living of their inhabitants. Social service provision increasingly dealt with the Inner City, but, even this was not enough either as a means of general welfare provision or of social control and when, with the onset of recession, British cities rioted in 1980 and 1981, the question was raised as to whether the American experience of 1967 was to be repeated across Europe.

7

The racial dimension was also present in Britain as it was to some extent in other European countries. Economic growth coupled with emigration during the fifties and sixties meant that inevitably the cities had to recruit immigrant populations to man the least desired jobs. To some extent this need was met by the migration of other Europeans from the poorer Southern European countries, but Britain, France, Belgium and Holland at least turned to their former colonial territories or to the colonial territories of other powers for migrants. In Britain this meant drawing on her own Deep South in the Caribbean as well as on the much more complexly structured and diverse populations of the Indian sub-continent. All the European nations had 'immigrant problems'. Britain in particular thought of itself as having a racial problem.

European societies and cities seemed at first to have an advantage over the United States. Even under Conservative administrations they were not likely to be so completely at the mercy of the 'natural laws' of capitalism. Cities were subject to planning regulation and a substantial part of the population lived in publicly provided rented housing. But urban sociological processes do not cease in the Welfare State. The decisons of the planning authorities themselves were constrained by economic and cultural imperatives. The population was being rehoused where land was cheapest, new industry located in the suburban fringe and new towns and public housing followed rather than resisting the suburban trend. The development of the Inner City remained a problem, albeit one which was in principle subject to public control. The 'Council House' in public suburbia was an ideal for many working class families in Britain, but such housing could not be provided immediately for all, and an alternative system had to be provided for those who were left behind.

The territorial segregation of the population between 'Inner City' and suburbs in part reflected and in part reinforced or produced strains in the dispensation of the Welfare State. In Britain at least therefore the policy responses which emerged were twofold. On the one hand there were a series of measures designed to plug the gaps in social services. On the other there were attempts to rectify the inequalities created by territorial and physical differences.

Under the first heading the strains were noticed first in the schools. An enquiry into the state of schools (Central Advisory Council 1968) showed that certain schools, particularly in, but not solely confined to, the inner city, were starved of resources, showed high indices of pathology and were likely to produce poor results. Thus it was decided that educational priority areas or educational priority schools should benefit from 'positive discrimination' with financial inducements being offered to place teachers and other non-human resources there. But the problem was by no means confined to the schools and by the end of the sixties a more general and very experimental community development programme was set in train. An Urban Programme administered by the Home Office was set up to finance new projects which would not have been encompassed by normal provision, and, in a few chosen areas, teams of social workers and researchers were implanted to undertake action research to find out and provide for undisclosed needs in the grass-roots communities.

Other initiatives, however, related to the physical fabric itself. Some of the old slum areas had disappeared by the late sixties and their former inhabitants had been transferred either to the suburbs or to redeveloped inner areas which sought to combine the advantages of high density high rise tower blocks with the more romantic cottagey suburban ideal. Resources ran out as far as the next worst housing was concerned, however, and it was decided that this housing should, so far as possible, not be replaced but improved (Department of the Environment 1968). Private householders and landlords were given substantial grants to provide

8

these houses with basic facilities and non-profit housing associatons went ahead with government help to carry out a programme of conversions of old houses into new homes. With this, the local authorities also undertook such measures as they could to improve streets rather than houses.

The hope was in these housing and area improvement schemes that the quality of life in the improvement areas could be made comparable with that of the suburbs and the inequality of condition between inner city and suburban citizens overcome. For a number of reasons this was difficult to achieve. The improvement areas took a long time to improve and the scars of the transition (e.g. boarded up houses and vacant sites awaiting redevelopment) themselves created a depressing atmosphere. The recent history of the decline of the areas also weighed too heavily for the possibility of a new future to be accepted. And, since not all of the pathologies of these areas were environmental, they were likely to retain a stigma even in the face of actual physical improvement. Nonetheless change was being achieved and, given sufficient resources, there was some sign by the late seventies that from an environmental point of view the improvement areas were improving. There was in fact nothing like the scene in inner city Chicago where the abandonment of site and buildings reduced large areas to looking like bomb-sites without the benefit of bombing and where any change depended upon property speculators who might seize on a particular area for 'gentrification'.

Another feature of the European as opposed to the American situation was the recognition that the improvement of the environment itself could not be accomplished without an improvement of employment prospects. The location of employment had long been a matter for public intervention and in the immediate post-war period the powers of central and local government had actually been used to direct industry away from the city centre to the suburban periphery and to wholly new towns. Those same powers could not be used to bring industry back and, if such pressure was beyond the capacity of local government, central government could intervene giving its authority to local Councils trying to revitalise the economy of declining areas. This was the aim of the Partnershp Authorities set up to bring together both Central and Local government initiatives and the separate activities of the Departments of the Environment and Industry as set out in a White Paper Policy for the Inner Cities in 1977 (Department of the Environment 1977a).

One remaining and glaring defect of the new policy was that the bringing together of industrial and environmental policy still left out any successful integration of educational services into the new plans. The environment and the industrial base were to be improved and strengthened. But it was widely believed that, insofar as any success was achieved in these ways, the new houses would have to be inhabited and the new industries would have to be manned by a different population. Little attention was given to the possibility that, through the retraining of adults and by the development of good schools for their children, the existing inner city population could have their lives improved. What seemed to be being proposed therefore was a reconquest of the inner city by the stable and secure working classes, a form, in fact, of public gentrification which was the socialist welfare state alternative to the kind of private gentrification which went on in countries where the control of land and houses was more at the mercy of private capitalism.

A quite different set of problems, however also had its effect on the development of these new social policies. It could rarely be publicly acknowledged as existing in a formally democratic society and had, in fact, to be concealed, to remain as a hidden agenda, in many policy arguments. But it was

9

there and it was the set of problems the attempt to solve which was actually determining decisions. In fact there were contradictions in other policies which made no sense unless it was realised that something else was at stake. This was the problem of the immigrant underclass, its interests, its struggles and the dangers it was perceived to represent. In the British case this took the form of an underlying racist anxiety.

Policy on the question of the rights of ethnic minorities and on their relation with the not very correctly called 'host society' had been the subject of separate legislation. All countries which had called in an immigrant labour force in times of prosperity later developed immigration control policies, partly in response to recession, but partly also in response to electoral xenophobia and racism. In the British case emphasis was placed upon restricting immigration from what was euphemistically called the New Commonwealth (Home Office 1965), while allowing it to continue freely from Ireland and making it even more possible for 'Patrials' (i.e. those with long-standing family connectons with Britain) and for citizens of the European Community. Such legislation served permanently to put in doubt the rights of immigrants. In Europe, of course, the situation of immigrants was often even more precarious because they were foreign nationals.

Contradicting these tendencies, however, was another new theme of legislation. This concerned the establishment of equal rights for the minorities. Legislation in Britain in 1965, 1968 and 1976 sought to resist discrimination on racial grounds through the setting up of a variety of new agencies working in conjunction with the courts, but also through conciliation. The difficulties with this legislation however were fourfold. There was no written constitution like that in the United States which could provide a basis for argument against discrimination. The judges and the public provided no legal and moral backing for the legislation. The resources devoted to the implementation of the policy were pitifully inadequate. And the separate service departments did not themselves build a concern with the 'ethnic dimension' into their policies. The result was that discrimination remained widespread and other departments, such as that of the Department of the Environment, denied that they had responsibilities in this area.

What had emerged, nonetheless, by the late seventies was a new set of priorities in social policy, which, although they had developed ad hoc were concerned to deal more flexibly and more comprehensively with the multitude of social problems especially amongst the urban poor which had not been provided for by the broad structure of the Welfare State as it has developed after 1945. These policies, however, were now subject to new strains, and, as the strains developed their inadequacies became more obvious.

The main source of strain was the onset of economic recession, particularly after 1979. If the Inner City Policy had been based upon the notion of re-directing investment, it was not clear what could be done when investment as such ceased to occur. As unemployment mounted in all countries, reaching a formally recognised figure of three million in Britain in 1982, there seemed little prospect of providing sufficient employment anywhere and not only in the inner city. Few new jobs became available for school-leavers. Even fewer of these appeared in the Inner City and, least of all were there likely to be jobs for Blacks and immigrants in a growing climate of racism. If, moreover, the wider problem in the sixties had been to extend the rights of the Welfare State to all, what now seemed to be called into question were these welfare rights themselves. In the sphere of housing, for example, the problem of ensuring minorities (and not only ethnic minorities) equality of access to public housing, was now submerged in that of whether the mainstream working class could rely on such housing.

10

The failure of the new policy dispensation to deal adequately enough or rapidly enough with the new circumstances was soon signalled, not merely by increasing poverty and despair in increasing sections of the population, but in rising rates of crime and, in the British case, in widespread civil disturbances involving a semi-military confrontation with the police.

The British riots of 1981 and 1982 did not start as a rising of the unemployed young poor or of the inner city population as a whole. They started with two separate types of confrontation between ethnic minorities and the police. On the one hand the young unemployed Black population of Brixton, mainly the children of West Indian immigrants, began to resist the heavy policing which had been the response to rising rates of street crime. On the other hand the Asian-descended population of Southall asserted their right to fight back against Fascist marches and widespread attacks by young White unemployed youths mobilised through various deviant youth cultures (e.g. some groups amongst the so-called Skinheads).

Having started in this way, however, the riots quickly spread to other areas and to other groups in the population. The long established British Blacks of Liverpool, together with some White youths, also began to confront the police in riot situations, and, in dozens of other centres, Black and White youth alike rioted in what were inadequately described as copy-cat riots.

After the riots three questons called for an answer. How far was the rioting due especially to problems affecting the immigrant minorities or to the failure of British society to incorporate its immigrant minorities adequately? How far was it due to the increasingly harsh conditions under which young people lived owing to the collapse of the economy and of existing social policies? And, finally, how far was it due to the failure of the police to be able to cope sensitively and adequately with a new social and political situation?

The official answer to the problem was a confused one. It was defined primarily as a law and order problem and, in contrast to the United States where the Kerner Commission on the disturbances of 1967 used social science evidence to focus on social causes and on racism and racial discrimination, the British Government appointed a single judge of the High Court to investigate the policing problem (Scarman 1981). Only as an afterthought did it ask this judge to go well beyond his competence and to comment on the social causes. Moreover the 'ethnic dimension' and the problems of race relations and racism were not explicitly faced at all.

What was apparent in this response was that, whatever the high aims of social policy, when it came to the crunch, the problem of the inner cities was a policing problem, whether this involved massive and heavy policing of a quasi-military sort or the softer style of community policing in which police gained the confidence of the community through providing for and controlling its social needs.

In fact the attempt by Lord Scarman to provide a recipe for sensitive policing, which would ensure the success of the fight against crime and yet preserve 'public tranquillity' has not met with universal acceptance. The police have not yet accepted that the methods which they use, particularly in policing the Black community, require fundamental alteration. At best they regard the Scarman recommendations as a tiresome constraint to which they have to adjust. So long as this is the case, then, one must assume that the inner city areas will go on being policed without the sensitivity and restraint which Scarman called for. It would seem that in times of crisis it is not to be social policy as such but rather control by force through which the 'inner-city' problem is to be managed.

There has, however, also been a response to the riots on the level of social policy, and this has been broadly twofold. On the one hand there has been a renewed concern with unemployment and with managing the young unemployed. On the other there has been a revival of interest in Inner City Policy.

The employment and unemployment response has itself been twofold. It has been concerned with providing for young people who have left school and have not found jobs through a new type of institutional arrangement intermediate between education and employment which might merely involve constructive use of time under supervision, but which might involve work-experience and training short of actual employment in a job. On the other hand it has been concerned with developing forms of economic activity, beyond those provided by larger employers, through small businesses, through self-employment, and even by positive encouragement of what was once thought of as the 'black' or 'hidden' economy.

These measures are far from adequate. So-called Youth Opportunity Schemes were originally posed as means of coping with transitional unemployment and cannot bear the strain of becoming a main means of providing for the young, unless they are fundamentally transformed to become serious means of education and training. The likelihood is that there will be serious tensions if not disturbances within these schemes unless they move in this direction. So far as smaller enterprises are concerned, it would seem that, with the exception of Asian business, which survives and grows on the basis of small profit margins, much of what is suggested seems like wishful thinking. Neither Youth Opportunities or Small Business development can take the strain of being called upon to provide economic revival. To the contrary they themselves can work effectively only as that revival occurs.

On the Inner City front, the Conservative Government in Britain was originally less than enthusiastic about a policy which seemed to depend too much on government intervention, government aid and government expenditure. The riots, however, have thrown doubt upon a policy of benign neglect and reliance on spontaneous enterprise. Conservatism has therefore developed its own Inner City style. It has sought to stimulate private initiative rather than relying on its spontaneous occurrence, both through the establishment of private enterprise zones, where normal government interference is withdrawn to encourage initiative, and by actively bringing together private businesses to push them towards Inner City investment. There has now developed a greater understanding of the fact that such development must be directed to the people who actually live in the Inner City, because, if it is not, they will riot, but it is still far from the case that education and training resources are being provided or racial and other forms of discrimination being resisted in ways which will ensure that they will benefit from such development as may occur.

Above all, it has to be noted, that, with the spread of rioting beyond the ethnic minority areas, the special problems and grievances of these minorities have been largely overlooked. The crisis of the Inner City has been redefined in traditional terms as a problem of employment and a problem of the environment. No major initiative has been directed to ensuring that the incorporation of ethnic minorities into British society either on a pluralistic basis or on the basis of assimilation. The one initiative which might have had a bearing on this, the setting up of a Commission of Enquiry into the position of minority children in schools, seemed by 1984 to have run into the ground or to be on the point of disintegration through acrimonious debates about whether the alleged failure of West-Indian descended children is the 'fault' of their families and community or the 'fault' of racist teachers in the schools (Department of Education and Science 1981).

Britain is, of course, just one amongst many European countries. Its problems, however, are not unique. They are problems of urban and industrial change which are shared by other European countries. All are likely to suffer from similar problems as the recession bites. It may well be the case therefore that just as Britain was once the exemplar of economic and industrial growth so now it may be the exemplar of advanced conditions of economic and political crisis. Other countries might take warning from the severity of the problems which confront it.

The account of social policy given here is, of course, the plainly pessimisitc diagnosis of a social scientist who is not in a position of having to develop policies ad hoc and to take respnsibility for them. It argues, first that the Welfare State or Beveridge dispensation provided only a broad framework for policy and was placed under considerable strain even in times of relative prosperity. It considers the attempts which were made to close the gaps in the sixties and seventies, but argues that these could not take the strain which recession and developing racial conflict imposed on the system by the late seventies. Finally, it considers the ad hoc responses to the riots and finds them falling short of a comprehensive and adequate set of politics.

To such a diagnosis those in responsible positions are likely to reply, 'It is easy for you to talk in this way, but what should we actually do? Would it not be better if you gave us credit for what we were doing and suggest improvements?' One understands this response and even sympathises with it. But it is not the task of social science to provide happy endings. If present policies are inadequate, or if they seem to point only to unresolved problems and further conflict, the social scientist has a duty to show that those problems will remain and those conflicts continue. It is not his duty to support wishful thinking or to bolster the confidence of those responsible for inadequate ad hoc arrangements.

What can be done is to suggest the areas in which policy development must go on these present ad hoc arrangements. These would seem to be as follows:

1. There must be a continuing recognition that the Welfare State dispensation provided only a broad framework for social policy and that it has continually to be improved to meet the real needs of disadvantaged minorities of all kinds.
2. It must be recognised that this is not simply an environmental problem, a territorial one, or purely a question of the level of economic activity.
3. It has nonetheless to be realised that there are problems of environmental improvement and problems of relating homes to jobs through industrial location or through efficient and cheap transport.
4. Education and training have to be provided sensitively to ensure that the poor and disadvantaged can take advantage of any programme of social and economic development.
5. Policies have to be developed to ensure that ethnic minorities are not forced into the position of an underclass whose sole relation to the society turns on their confrontation with the police.
6. It must be recognised that present rates of unemployment lead dangerously towards reliance on policies of control rather than welfare and that far more has to be done by way of genuine training and retraining, and through normal educational provision, to ensure a future for disadvantaged groups rather than merely keeping them off the streets.
7. Inner City and other similar policies have to be rewritten so that they start with the needs of the people rather than simply furthering the policy imperatives of a particular department.
8. The task of policing should be that of providing a framework within which life and liberty can be preserved while allowing for the normal development of

political conflict and political change. It cannot itself be responsible for social policy or government.

Behind all of these policy developments, however, lies the problem of the present economic crisis and of the possibility or otherwise of economic recovery. That is not a matter for the expert on social policy. All he or she can say is that present levels of unemployment are producing nearly irresolvable problems and that if they are sustained they are likely to lead in one direction or another to the abandonment of our democratic life in favour of some more authoritarian form. Possibly the problem of unemployment will have to be resolved in part by job division and job sharing. That might reduce the actual divisions which have been opened up by the recession. In the meanwhile what can be discussed in social policy are the ways in which those who appear to have lost out in the present struggle for survival can have a fair chance of and can in any case develop their skills, their dignity and their political capacity so that they can resist other more authoritarian solutions to their problems which are presently on offer.

II   Social policy and ethnic inequality

Stages of race relations policy

It was suggested by Nicholas Deakin (Deakin 1970) that British policy on race relations had gone through three stages. The first was a policy of laissez faire in which racial distinctions were not recognised; the second was one of increasing racialist practice; while the third was one in which serious attempts were made to grapple with the problem. That was 1969. Looking back with the benefit of fifteen years more hindsight it is possible to distinguish extra stages. What Deakin called the 'liberal hour' did not strike in 1968. What happened was the development of race relations policies and social policy generally in two divergent directions. One the one hand there was an escalation of racist ideology, signalled by the Powell speech of 1968. On the other there was an attempt to deal with racial injustice and inequality by stealth, including it under a wider and more diffuse heading of 'disadvantage'. When, however, Britain experienced her Watts riots in St. Paul's, Bristol in 1980 and her 'long hot summer' of 1981, these policies were shown to be inadequate. The political power of minorities began to assert itself both on the streets and through the ballot box and there was a political response in terms of 'equal opportunity' and 'multi-racial' policies whose impact we are only beginning to experience.

The stages I would suggest are thus are different from Deakins. I shall ignore the stages of laissez faire, since it was an ideal for dealing with black men and women only so long as they lived thousands of miles away. The first stage of policy for British Blacks was one of structural racism in which building on a basis of racially selective immigration policy, barriers were set up, which ensured the inequality of Black people who had managed to settle in all the main institutional spheres, but particularly in employment, housing and education. The second stage was that in which any special problem was denied and in which it was argued that, if the main thrust of our policy was to correct the deprivation of our urban disadvantaged poor, racial injustice would disappear. The third stage, now beginning, is that in which the minorities have asserted themselves and there are the beginnings of policies based upon the possibly contradictory notions of 'equal opportunity' and 'multi-culturalism'. Such policies at the moment are both minimal and crude. It is possible that they will both produce a White backlash and yet fail to satisfy minority demands for equality. In that case there will be a further stage either of escalation of racist politics or alternately institutions promoting racial equality established and defended from positions of political power.

The stage of racialist reaction

I am not one of those who holds that advanced industrial and semi-planned societies can be expected to dispense with an immigration policy. The most, I think that can be asked for is what was suggested at a recent conference on humane options in immigration policy, namely, that the richer countries could be expected to include in such policies a 'category of generosity' through which such countries allowed, in addition to the immigration which was necessary to meet their economic needs, for a small additional number of immigrants in order to relieve the poverty of the Third World (Fried 1983). Unfortunately, however, British immigration policy does not begin to measure up to these standards. There is not and never has been 'a category of generosity'. Still worse, it can be argued, Britain has never developed an immigration policy at all. It has allowed Irish, E.E.C. and Old White Commonwealth immigration to go on almost without control, but it has devised means whereby, those of darker skin colour are excluded, whether or not their skills and abilities are of use to Britain.

However much social policy became more anti-racialist during the sixties and early seventies, immigration policy became more and more explicitly racialist. The original act limiting Commonwealth immigration applied at least in theory to all Commonwealth immigrants Black and White alike, but thereafter changes were introduced which progressively directed the controls against Black and Asian immigrants. The 1968 Act extended the original controls to British passport holders who were not patrials (especially of course, the East African Asians who had opted for British citizenship) and the principle of patriality became the basis for admission and inclusion in the 1971 Act. Ironically it was James Callaghan who had introduced the 1968 Act who pointed out that the 1971 Act was not really an act of Immigration Control at all, since it greatly increased the numbers of those having a right of settlement i.e. through recognising the right of patrials to be exempt from immigration control. What he was recognising at this point was that immigration policy had been replaced by a policy of purely racial exclusion.

Two views were expressed as to the effect of racial immigration control in the 60's. One was that of Roy Hattersley that 'Integration without control is impossible, though control without integration is morally indefensible'. The other was that of Archbishop Ramsey who, on assuming the Chairmanship of the National Committee for Commonwealth Immigration warned that he might have to return to the government to tell it that racial immigration control was itself damaging to minorities, and that, so long as it existed, integration was impossible. In fact it was Hattersley's view, or at least the first part of it that prevailed. The Archbishop's N.C.C.I. broke up through resignations at the time of the 1968 Act and was replaced by the much more politically ambiguous Community Relations Commission.

Whether the warning implicit in the second part of the Hattersley formula was heeded can only be judged from the record of what happened by way of discrimination and disadvantage to the Asian, E. African and Caribbean settlers in the spheres of employment, housing and education.

So far as employment was concerned, David Smith's 'Racial disadvantage in

Britain' based on the second P.E.P. study (Smith 1977) is still the best source. It shows that although superficially the social class and occupational distribution of the Indian and East African Asians approximated to those of the British, Asians and West Indians were overwhelmingly concentrated in those jobs which were marked by heavy work, shift work and low wages. The problem of promotion was particularly acute and, as the Mansfield Hosiery Dispute, the Imperial Typewriter Dispute and other similar disputes showed, Asian and West Indian workers were inadequately protected by their unions and opposed by their White fellow workers when they tried to enter better paid jobs. So far as unemployment was concerned, while prosperity lasted, Black and Asian unemployment rates came to approximate those of White, but, as unemployment rose, it was disproportionately for Asians and Blacks and, above all, amongst young British born blacks. By the 80's it was normal in inner cities for well over half of the young Black population to be unemployed.

Turning to housing, in the 1960's the two normal sources of housing improvement, namely Council Housing and purchase with the aid of mortgages, were largely closed to those West Indians and Asians who sought to use them. They therefore turned to an alternative system provided in the first place by immigrant landlords and then by Council mortgages or inner city property and Housing Association tenancies. True, the 1968 Race Relations Act made the wider forms of discrimination by Councils, Building Societies, Estate Agents and vendors illegal, but the Act took a long time to have effect, and by that time segregated immigrant communites had been established. The result was increasing segregation in inner city wards (Birmingham, for example, by 1981 had 6 wards with more than 48% of their population living in households with a New Commonwealth or Pakistani head). Such segregation did depend in part on choice as well as constraint, but it is not true that either Asians or West Indians chose to be segregated in the worst Inner City housing.

Finally, educational segregation followed housing segregation. If a ward had, say, 60% of its population living in N.C.W.P. households, more than 90% of the children at school would be drawn from this group, since the 40% of Whites would consist very largely of old people, whose children and grandchildren had migrated to the suburbs, or Irish who sent their children to Catholic schools. While these Black and Asian schools received additional aid after the mid-sixties there is no reason to suppose that there is anything in the British experience to controvert the Brown versus the Board of Education judgement in the United States that such segregated education is inherently unequal. Moreover even those Black and Asian children who found their way to less segregated schools still faced disadvantage. Their real linguistic problems and family problems, could not be dealt with without specialised resources, and it was all too easy to see them as remedial or disciplinary cases.

The second P.E.P. study and a host of official and unofficial reports captured the degrees of disadvantage suffered by minorities in quantitative terms. What was more important than quantitative disadvantage, however, was the structural division which was being opened up in British society. Though Black and Asian workers joined trades unions and some did succeed in getting in better jobs, or in resisting proletarianisation through ethnic business, the fact was that there was a division in the labour market between the nature of employment available to Black and Asian workers and the jobs sought and filled by native British. Segregation in terms of housing actually increased sharply between 1971 and 1981 and was intensified by White flight, and the largely Black school provided the normal environment for the children of West Indians and Asians.

Myrdal had suggested (Myrdal 1964) that in a competitive and individualistic

17

society like that of the U.S.A. poor Blacks tended to drop out of the system and to become an 'underclass' characterised by a culture of poverty, by a tangle of pathologies tranmitted from generation to generation and by increasing unemployment and unemployability. This was not exactly true in Britain. Society here was not structured so much on the basis of competitive individualism. What the working class had won in Britain was a certain right to security of employment, to welfare benefits and to rights in the spheres of housing health and education. But it was precisely in relation to these rights that Black and Asian workers were excluded. A relatively privileged working class, at least in times of prosperity, excluded Black and Asians from full participation in its privileges. To that extent Black and Asian workers were placed in an underclass situation. They did not necessarily become the kind of rotting mass which Myrdal described, however. What they did was to develop their own politics, culture and organisation, based partly upon resistance and political struggle and partly on the maintenance of links with their homelands. It was this process of political struggle which was eventually to lead to the third stage to which I refer, namely that of equal opportunity policies (Rex and Tomlinson 1979).

Before I go on to discuss the second and third stages, however, there is one other point which has to be made. This is that the political and structural position of a minority group depends not simply on its participation in social benefits. It also rests upon the access which such a group has to protection by the primary institutions of law and order. That is to say it depends upon the day-to-day treatment of the minority group by the police.

What clearly did not happen in the sphere of policing was the enunciation of any clear policy asserting the legal right of the minorities to equal treatment. Instead, two things happened. One was that, failing even remotely to understand the culture and the social and political aspirations of West Indian youth, and bringing to their task archaic colonialist attitudes, the police saw the very existence of these youths as a threat to law and order and adopted those forms of heavy policing which the West Indian community saw as harassment. The other was that they failed to give protection to the minority communities, and especially the Asian community, against physical and political attack. Thus the minority communities were seen as outlaws, either engaged in open struggle with the police themselves or inadequately protected by the police against organised or spontaneous racism.

Policing, of course, is not thought of as one of the main aspects of social policy and, indeed, the form of policing which we have is not closely directed by government either at national or local level. Nonetheless the form of policing which government allows by default crucially determines the possibility of integration. Not surprisingly, therefore, it was the encounter between the police and the minorities which came crucially to determine changes in policy in the long run.

All in all what one saw as the first stage of policy development, then was a racialist reaction to the presence of minorities. They were not seen as citizens with normal social and political and legal rights, but rather as outsiders who had no real right to be here in Britain. It was this sentiment which led, however much he sought to deny racialist intent, to the widespread popular support for Enoch Powell's speech in 1968.

Policies for the 'disadvantaged'

Those who made social policy, of course, did not explicitly adopt racial discrimination and harassment as a policy. But they did not recognise it and seek to combat it either. Rather they argued that the problem was not one of racialism in British politics or the British electorate, but the existence of something already well understood, namely inequality and disadvantage. Immigration it was often said constituted the 'barium meal' of British society and the task was to deal not with the symptoms but with the underlying disease. Fabians saw it as reinforcing their own long-standing campaign for greater social equality. Marxists saw it as yet another indictment of capitalism. What I wish to argue here, however, is that however great the case for greater social equality may be and however evil the consequences of capitalism, structural racism had its own dimensions and that the attempt to incorporate it under the heading of the more general category of 'disadvantage' often involved no more than what a colleague of mine has called 'the deracialisation of racist discourse' (Reeves 1983).

My own first encounter with the new approach to minority problems which emerged in the sixties was as a member of the Housing Panel of the National Community for Commonwealth Immigrants. I had wanted the Committee to deal with the clear and simple issues of racial discrimination, whether direct or indirect, in the business of housing, particularly in the public sector, and I argued this case as best I could in the committee. What eventually emerged in the N.C.C.I., however, was simply a pamphlet on 'Areas of Special Housing Need' (N.C.C.I. 1967). The argument was that it was not so much racialist policies which were the heart of the problem. It was not that minorities were living and forced to live in the worst and more rapidly decaying inner city area, but rather that those areas existed at all. Typically, therefore, attention was diverted away from the specific issue of racialism to more general and comfortably understood issues of social reform.

Perhaps, however, the problem was not that these issues were comfortably understood. What was happening in the sixties was the discovery that the orthodox policies of social welfare were not working for a large minority of the population. The work of Peter Townsend and others had led to the discovery that the Welfare State was not working and there was a new crusade to extend social policy to cover the problems of the so-called New Poor. This, was of course, a noble crusade, and one with which I would wish to be associated in every way. In this context, however, its existence made my problem more difficult, because for many the crusade on behalf of the New Poor included all things and structural racism was seen as something which would automatically disappear, if only we dealt effectively with the problems of disadvantage.

The new theme of 'disadvantage' first emerged in the thinking of government departments with the publication of the Plowden and Newsom reports (Central Advisory Council for Education 1967, 1968). Inner-city and working-class schools were seen as imposing grave disadvantages on their children and positive discrimination in the allocation of resources was recommended in favour, first of areas, then of schools marked by certain indices of disadvantage. Far from any special problem of disadvantage experienced by minority children being diagnosed, however, the very presence of minority children in the school was one of the indices of disadvantage, presumably for the White children.

A similar approach was adopted more generally by the Labour Government of 1964. Harold Wilson and Richard Crossman responded to the racial hostility to the pressure of Black and Asian immigrants in the cities, by arguing that the real problem of those cities lay in their deficient social services. They therefore proposed that the cities should benefit from special economic aid. True, in the Local Government Act of 1966 they provided in Section 11 for additional aid, where the arrival of immigrants had presented new problems. But the aid was to be given to areas and institutions rather than to the minorities themselves. Once again the presence of immigrants was seen as a symptom of disadvantage rather than as raising new problems of combatting discrimination.

The 'long hot summer' of 1968 in the United States produced further reactions along the same lines. The Home Office now entered the scene with is own proposals for dealing with poverty through an 'Urban Programme' designed to help 'projects' which arose to assist the urban poor. Beyond this, and in more radical vein it set up the Community Development Projects to diagnose and suggest provision for the disadvantaged.

Other developments occurred in other departments. The Select Committee on Immigration which dealt with the problems of West Indian school-leavers (Select Committee 1969) had suggested that there should be a special centre to consider what their resource needs were. The Department of Education and Science responded to this simply by setting up the Centre for Educational Disadvantage in Manchester, claiming that this was sufficient to provide for immigrant needs. Meanwhile in the Department of Health and Social Security, Sir Keith Joseph, inspired no doubt by the Moynihan Report in the United States, commissioned a series of studies on Transmitted Deprivation.

More important than any of these developments, however, was the new focus on what came to be called 'The Inner City'. Mr. Peter Walker who was the Conservative Minister at the Department of the Environment and who was deeply impressed by developments in the United States, had risked unpopularity by raising in a series of speeches the twin problems of the deterioration of the Inner City and unemployment amongst Black youth. As Secretary of State, therefore, he commissioned three Inner City studies in Lambeth, Small Heath and Liverpool 8 (Department of the Environment 1977b). These led in due course, under his successor, Mr. Peter Shore to the White Paper Policy for the Inner Cities (Department of the Environment 1977a).

Unfortunately, by the time the White Paper had emerged thinking had moved away from the specific problems of Black Youth unemployment which Mr. Walker had sought to raise. The White Paper explicity denied that it was concerned with questions of racial inequality and proposed bringing together the work of the Departments of Trade and Industry and the Environment and Central and Local Government in new Urban Partnerships. These partnerships would treat the problem of the Inner City as one of poverty and would seek to ensure that the economic as well as the environmental decline of the Inner City was arrested.

The White Paper however, did not go as far as some other policy initiatives even in dealing with the problems of the disadvantaged poor. In putting forward its proposals for economic revitalisation it did not necessarily argue that these proposals should benefit the existing inner city residents. In a curious section on population movements it argued that, if revitalisation occurred, the existing population, who were often unskilled or retired, should be encouraged to move to the periphery.

Had this policy really been implemented and had the recession not withdrawn the resources necessary for its success, therefore, there is no guarantee that either the inner city poor or the Black and Asian immigrants would have benefitted. The main provision made for them was not to be in the main programmes, but rather in the marginal Urban Programme for which the Partnerships were now given responsibility. A great deal of subsequent discussion of the position of Ethnic Minorities was therefore devoted to the question of the share of those minorities in the Urban Programme.

The Inner City Policy, in fact, serves nicely to illustrate the mischievous way in which minority problems were avoided by including them under the heading of 'disadvantage'. Whatever might be true of the White residents of the Inner City, it was not true that the minorities consised simply of unskilled people. Much of the evidence suggested that, whatever jobs they were currently doing, the minority populations represented an untapped reservoir of skills and qualifications, especially so far as the Asian population was concerned. It was clear, moreover, that the children of these immigrants could, if given adequate education, become precisely the sort of skilled labour force which a revitalised inner city would need. By including them all under the heading of those who were disadvantaged because they were unskilled, therefore, the White Paper simply evaded the problem of racial discrimination and of the inadequacy of the social services available specifically to immigrants and their children.

I hope I have made it clear that the development of social policy in the 1960's, progressive though it was in many respects did not in fact deal with the deep divisions which were opening up in British society between the host population and the Black and Asian minorities. By pretending that it did many of us have helped only to conceal the problem. The extent to which it did was revealed when Britain's cities exploded in 1980 and 1981.

Policies to combat racial discrimination

Naturally, in any schematic review of policy such as this, I have left out certain other developments. I now want to add that there were policy initiatives in the 1960's and 1970's designed to deal more specifically with the deepening social divisions in our society. I shall also argue, however, that these policies were against the mainstream and were marginalised and ineffective until the urban disturbances of 1981 which shattered the complacency of policy makers.

Right back into the 1950's there had been opposite thrusts in political and policy thinking about race. Mr. Cyril Osborne had campaigned in Parliament for racially selective immigration control. But on the other hand Fenner Brockway and Reginald Sorenson had presented Bill after Bill to outlaw racial discrimination. It was the Osborne policy which first came to fruition in 1962 and, as is well known, despite Gaitskell's commitment to reverse the Immigration Control Act of 1962, the Wilson government came to accept it and indeed to strengthen it. At the same time, however, it took the first token steps in 1965 to implement Brockway's policy. The Hattersley formula of 'No Integration without Control, but no Control without Integration' summed up and sought to synthesise these dialectically opposed trends.

There is no need here to go into great detail on the 1965 and 1968 Race Relations Acts. The first was defective in that it applied only to public places and left out discrimination in crucial areas such as housing and employment. The second, while covering these areas, failed to make adequate provision for implementation and also provided for many loopholes and exceptions. By 1976, however, much experience had been gained and in many respects the new Act of that year was a strong Act by comparable American standards.

Three things stand out in the provisions of the 1976 Act. It recognised in terms of a tight definition the existence of indirect discrimination. It gave the initiative to the new Commission for Racial Equality in bringing cases before tribunals and in carrying out its own investigations. And it called upon, though it did not require, Local Authorities to implement Equal Opportunity Policies.

21

Of course there were many structural and political factors preventing the Act from being fully effective. It is doubtful whether it could best achieve its new and stronger aims when the work of the old Race Relations Board was merged with the goodwill-promoting work of the Community Relations Commission. The investigations were carried out by a derisorily small staff and could be expected to have little more than an educational effect. And, so far as the Local Authorities were concerned, so long as Section 71 of the Act was not mandatory, it seemed unlikely that many of them would do anything about it. All of these elements of the legislation could, however, be made effective given the necessary political will, and even if that will was not present at the highest political level, matters were considerably changed by the disturbances of 1981 and departmental responses to them.

The disturbances of 1981

It is ironic that, although Mr. Peter Walker's Inner City Studies dealt with Lambeth, Small Heath and Liverpool 8 and were intended to deal with the looming problems of those areas and areas like them, it was in two of them that rioting actually broke out in 1981. If any evidence was needed to show that the Inner City Policy was not working this was it.

It is important, however, to make clear exactly what we mean when we say this. It is not that poor economic and environmental conditions inevitably lead to riot. The crucial linking element in a situation which leads to a break down of law and order and the use of violence must be that of the relations between people and the police. It is only when police actions as well as the policies which they enforce are no longer regarded as legitimate that riots occur. We must, therefore, give primary attention, as Lord Scarman was initially supposed to do, to police-community relations.

In fact Lord Scarman was ill-equipped, as any one man must have been, to deal with 'underlying social causes'. What his position enabled him to do was to analyse the policing process and more subtly to devise a package of proposals which might lead to reform in what is a largely independent organisation.

Scarman's proposals (Scarman 1981) have been criticised by radicals for their moderation and rightly so. What should not be overlooked however was that he was clear that the events in Brixton could not have occurred had police behaviour not been so inept and so implicity as well as overtly racist. He saw 'racism' as a problem at the level of recuitment, training and actual policing practice. He criticised the specific decisions to use heavy policing methods against the community, even if he admitted the necessity of police discretion in these matters and he argued for community policing of a kind. He argued for community liaison, even if he rejected accountability to local Councils. And he called for an independent element in the investigation of complaints against the police.

The police reaction to these suggestions appears to have been one of outrage and anger and it might have been expected perhaps that its effect would have been merely to reinforce their racism and their demand for independence. The report, however, did have the effect of challenging that independence and has enabled both external and internal critics of existing police practice to put the question of police reform and police responsibility to the community on the political agenda. Had this not been the case there might well have been an early recurrence of riots, since the so-called 'underlying social causes' have certainly become more acute since 1981. This is by no means to say that the reform of police behaviour towards minority communities has been anything like complete, but it has given a breathing space in which it has been possible to rethink other aspects of social policy.

So far as it itself, dealt with the underlying social causes of the Brixton riots, the Scarman tribunal in fact had little new to say. It noted the fact of ethnic minority disadvantage, but had little to say about ways of attacking it. What it did say, moreover, was wrong. On the one hand it misinterpreted the term 'institutionalised discrimination', taking it to mean legally sanctioned discrimination, and thus claimed that it did not exist in Britain. On the other it suggested that what was now needed was 'positive discrimination' implying that minorities had already been given rights, but now needed some special paternalistic intervention to enable them to achieve equality. On this second point, one Black leader is reported as saying with some point 'First you break our leg. Then you offer us a crutch'.

In fact the Scarman Report was not, as was often suggested a kind of new charter for race relations in Britain. It says something, indeed, of the racism of policy thinking that it should be thought to be so. It was only because Black and Asian immigrants were still thought of as a police problem that such a belief could even be canvassed. What was much more important for race relations than the Scarman Report was the direct effect of the riots on thinking about other issues of social policy. Conscious that they faced a minority electorate which was capable of voting as well as rioting, the local authorities which had dragged their feet over the implementation of Section 71 of the Race Relations Act now began to devise Equal Opportunity policies. It is to these policies, very different in conception from policies based upon the concept of generalised disadvantage, that we must now turn.

The local authorities and equal opportunity policy

The first response of many local authorities to the riots and to the pressure to implement Equal Opportunity Policies was simply to adopt token declarations. Those who had 'resisted' or 'wavered' about Section 71 (to use Ken Young's term) now declared themselves in favour of having a policy (Young and Connelly 1981). The question now, however, is not simply of whether the resistors and waverers adopt a policy, but what, having adopted a policy, they actually do. It is on our assessment of the effectiveness of these policies that our judgement as to whether we shall be able to create a racially and ethnically equal society must rest.

Since 'equal opportunity' by itself is simply an empty slogan what we should now be doing is looking at the kind and the scope of policies now being adopted by equal opportunity authorities to find out what it actually means in practice. At best, it would seem, it refers to the following aspects of local authority policies:-

(1)   A review of personnel practices by the authority itself as a major employer.

(2)   Monitoring the extent of employment of minority people in Local Authority jobs.

(3)   The creation of special Race Relations or Equal Opportunity Departments to advise on these matters.

(4)   Training of Officers in Racial and Ethnic awareness.

23

(5)   Equality of service delivery in spheres for which local authorities are responsible such as housing, education and the personal social services.

More progress has been made on the first four of these, since it is the Metropolitan Councils which have been most active in promoting Equal Opportunity policies and they do not have responsibility for service delivery.

Perhaps the least important initiatives have been those which have led to the creation of Equal Opportunity and Race Relations Departments. There is always the possibility that they will simply lead to the creation of jobs for Minority Race Relations professionals and that for these professionals the existence of their own jobs will be an end in itself. Nonetheless, even the pathological notion of 'Jobs for Ethnic Minority Boys (and Girls)' achieves something. At worst it recognises the right of Black people to top-paid jobs. At best it might mean that those concerned have the authority to impose a new constraint on policy making.

Much more important are initiatives arising under the headings (1) and (2) above. So called 'monitored percentages' have had a very useful effect in promoting racial equality in the United States and could also do so here. They do not imply positive discrimination in the unacceptable sense mentioned earlier. Nor do they imply the appointment of incompetents so that percentages can be attained. What they do mean is that the authority is committed to the idea that minorities should be adequately represented in its services and that it provides training to ensure that qualified candidates are available.

Without such training programmes the intervention of Equal Opportunity Policy and Race Relations officers in personnel matters can be a purely formal and token gesture. Too often in fact this appears to be what is happening. The Establishment and Personnel Departments are forced to comply with with certain formal standards set by Race Relations policy when they place the advertisement of a selection for posts but when it comes to appointment they can all too easily argue that ethnic minority candidates should not be appointed because of other criteria. At most therefore what Equal Opportunity Personnel policies have been able to achieve is an educative effect so that those who make appointments know that they cannot legitimately exclude candidates on ethnic or racial grounds.

Training Local Government employees in anti-racism presents more difficult problems. Such policies under the title of Racial and Ethnic Awareness have had some success in the United States as part of an overall Civil Rights Policy to which government at the highest level has become publicly committed, but no such situation exists in Britain. What can be the case is that in some local authorities there emerges an inter-party consensus on these matters and that employees who go to such courses know that it is in their career interests to accept them. If this is not the case, however, what is likely to happen is that courses will be accepted in an almost masochistic way with the students being fully aware that what they have to accept has no real legitimacy. In these cases it may be thought sufficient simply to bring in Minority tutors to berate White officers about their racism, but without any real change in policy being achieved.

Surprisingly little has been done so far to monitor local authority housing policies in the light of equal opportunity and the main areas of discussion regarding service delivery have been concerned with education and the personal social services. In these areas, however, the principle problem has been the equation of equal opportunity with multi-culturalism. This equation is not in fact a logical one and presents real problems.

When the U.N.E.S.C.O. Experts committee met to discuss the nature of racism and race prejudice in 1967 it specifically rejected the inclusion of a statement about 'the right to be different' (Montagu 1972). It did so because it seemed to the members that the inclusion of such a statement would be used by anti-egalitarian forces to justify almost any form of inequality. That which was different in social provision could also very easily be that which was inferior. These are relevant considerations when we come to consider proposals to implement equal opportunity policies through the provision of multi-cultural services.

It is true of course, that ethnic minorities are concerned that their specific ethnic needs should be provided for and that their culture should be respected. This has led some Muslim parents for example to demand separate Muslim schools. But no ethnic minority organisation has every suggested that the provision for such needs should take precedence over equality of educational opportunity. Equally in the British political debate when Roy Jenkins accepted the goal of multi-culturalism in opposition to the assimilationism of the Commonwealth Immigrants Advisory Council, he was careful to couple the notion with that of equality of opportunity.

There are within education and within the other social services many aspects of social provision which can help or hinder equal opportunity. In education, for example, there is a need for early instruction in the mother tongue, for effective mother tongue maintenance, for ESL provision at elementary and more sophisticated levels, for curricula which appeal to minorities because they are offered in genuine respect for their cultures, and for specific education in anti-racism, because all of these matters affect the capacity of minority children to compete in a highly competitive and credentialling system. If, then, this is what multi-cultural educational policy is about it must be welcomed as a proper implementation of equal opportunity policy.

Unfortunately this is not what is usually meant by multi-cultural education. Instead it has often been based upon on unproven psychological theory that immigrant children (especially West Indian children) have a low self-image which affects performance and that self-image can be improved by education in their own culture (Stone 1981). In fact the diagnosis is unproven and the cure likely to be ineffective - ineffective in any case but the more so when multi-cultural education involves little more than a token or paternalistic recognition of minority cultures in the low-status uncertificated parts of the curriculum, what some of us call the curriculum of the three S's - saris, samosas and steel bands. And it is multi-cultural education in this sense which has been the predominant doctrine which has prevailed even when it is offered in the name of equal opportunity.

Quite clearly educational achievement is of the essence of what equal opportunity requires and this means under our educational system achievement in a severely competitive system. The first necessity, therefore from a minority point of view is that minority children should be offered a good education in professional terms. Multi-cultural education can actually play a part within such an educational policy. But what is not acceptable is multi-culturalism taken by itself without regard to or at the expense of equality of opportunity.

Similarly provision within the personal social services requires a multi-cultural dimension. But it is not always a lack of this dimension which results in poor social services and poor social work. Very often these are poor because they are sub-professional. What is wanted is a raising of these standards, including of course a multi-cultural dimension. The mere introduction of multi-culturalism by itself is unlikely to ensure truly fair and equal treatment.

It is clear then that the problems implicit in Equal Opportunity policies have not yet been resolved. There are many confused ideas involved and there is always a danger of tokenism. What is important to notice however is that three years after the riots of 1981 a certain momentum has been created and that might count for more than the specific policies advocated. Certainly it is the case that, despite the absence of any political will on this matter at Central Government level, some local authorities have become committed to a policy of racial equality, and, backed as they are by a minority electorate, this may provide a genuine breakthrough against the development of structural racism in a way in which disadvantage policies never did.

Even this, however, may be untrue by, say, 1986, for the policies initiated since 1981 are now already running into a backlash. When, for example, a local authority requires its headteachers to go on anti-racist courses or introduces halal meat in the school meals service, there is an outcry well orchestrated by extreme right-wing and racist organisations and strongly supported in the local and popular national press. It remains to be seen whether such pressure will lead to a reversal of policies. Moreover the very authorities which have done most to pioneer equal opportunity policies, namely the Metropolitan Councils were abolished in 1986 partly because these policies are amongst those which have given most offence to the Conservative Government.

It must also be added that the Local Authorities cannot by themselves change British society. They are, it is true, very large employers but unless the policies which they have developed are also followed by Central Government and by industry their effect will at best be partial. Not least it is necessary that similar policies should be developed in relation to the police and the practice of policing. Sor far unfortunately Central Government has done little by way of monitoring its employment policies, only the largest firms have codes of practice on ethnic equality and those largely of a formalistic level, and, so far as the police are concerned, only the weakest possible forms of anti-racist training have been introduced. All of these are matters to be tackled if the possibility of structural racism is to be avoided. It has also to be noticed that all of these problems are greatly intensified by the onset of recession. Fortunately and contrary to expectation we have not therefore seen a major new emphasis on race in party politics. The heyday of racial mobilisation of the White electorate occurred in the years immediately after the Powell speech of 1968. Since then, despite the penetration of the Parliamentary Conservative Party by racist elements, race has largely dropped off the political agends. The major points of political confrontation have been directly concerned with class and the unions. It is far from the case, however, that racism has ceased to exist and it might well be that, as the recession deepens, there will be both spontaneous outburst of racist activity and an increasing backlash against the equal opportunity policies we have been discussing. For this reason it must be said that such policies have a precarious foundation.

Conclusion

What I have sort to argue here is that after an initial period of racialism in policy following the arrival of Black and Asian immigrants, Britain first sought to wish the problem away by defining it as part of the more readily and comfortably understood problem of disadvantage, but that these initial reactions were challenged by the riots of 1981 in a way which produced at least a limited attempt to address the specific problems of racial inequality. The political foundations of these policies, however, are profoundly insecure and we are only at the beginning of the fight to prevent the emergence of a structurally racist society.

26

One last point remains to be made lest I should be misunderstood. This is that in dissociating the specifically racial dimension from other forms of disadvantage and inequality, I am <u>not</u> saying that there is an ethnic dimension or a colour dimension in inequality which has nothing to do with class. What is happening is that the much more severe forms of class struggle generated by empire have now been superimposed upon domestic class politics. The question is whether the effective expression of minority political power may combine with universalistic traditions in British politics to ensure that we develop a concept of citizenship and social rights that does not rest upon race and racialism.

III   The segregation and integration of Britain's black minorities

The notion that the main choice which we have to make in Britain is simply between segregation and integration is a comforting and unchallenging one because it suggests that no questions of inequality, exploitation and oppression are involved. We seem simply to be called upon to decide between two cultural alternatives each with its own aesthetic attractions. What I want to discuss, however, and what has always been involved in the study of racial segregation, is basically a question of injustice betwen groups and one which can in fact only be resolved by political struggle by the oppressed and intelligent policy responses on the part of the state.

It is true, of course, that, when Britain chose to fill her labour gap in the fifties, not merely with Irish, who were actually the largest contingent of immigrants, and with Europeans fleeing from one or another sort of political oppression, but with recruits from the Caribbean and the Indian sub-continent, it tacitly accepted, through the failure to produce alternative policies, that dark-skinned immigrants would be housed in quasi-ghetto conditions, that they would be largely confined to the least wanted jobs, and that their children would be sent to school in ways which did least to disrupt normal English education. There is a sense therefore in which one could say that we now have a segregated Black and Asian population and the problem is that of whether they stay that way or are encouraged and allowed to enter main-stream society. But the essence of this problem is that of the nature of the barriers that stand in the way. We have to look at the complex of political and economic interests which stand in the way of integration rather than merely pretending that we have an easy moral and cultural choice.

The greatest of social scientists to write about race relations questions, Gunnar Myrdal, suggested as he looked at the ghettoes of New York in 1964 that the only appropriate term to describe the unemployed and largely black poor was a Swedish term which he translated as 'underclass' (Myrdal 1964). This underclass, he suggested, consisted of 'unemployed and gradually unemployable families at the bottom of a society, in which for the majority of people above that level, the increasingly democratic structure of the educational system creates more and more liberty... at least over the course of two generations'.

The basic model of society here suggested is that of a competitive and individualistic system in which the great majority of individuals are able to meet their needs and which they regard as legitimate because it allows this while at the same time maximising their own area of choice and freedom. The problem of the underlcass is that they no longer have the motivation to enter such a system. They remain caught up 'in a tangle of pathologies' living in a 'culture of poverty' and transmitting their deprivation to their children.

I have suggested many times that Myrdal's model is misleading if applied uncritically to Britain. It is misleading in that British society is not based upon that open and competitive system which Myrdal sees as operating in the mainstream of the United States and it is misleading in that our Black and Asian populations have not yet rotted in the ghetto for several generations and have certainly not become the kind of despairing mass which Myrdal sees as existing in the ghettoes of the United States.

The British mainstream in the fifties and the sixties was not basically a system of competitive individuallsm. Rather it was a system which had arisen out of class stuggle based upon solidarity and collective action to defend themselves against exploitation by the working class. So successful had this struggle been that, in the post-war dispensation, everyone was in principle entitled to certain social rights and both the major political parties were committed to the maintenance of full employment and to free collective bargaining. The system which British working class people regarded as legitimate therefore was not one in which all competed equally in the market place, but rather one in which, as a result of collective action, all enjoyed the basic rights of the Welfare State. In the main this bundle of rights had little to do with getting on or getting to the top. 'The poorest he', as Colonel Thomas Rainsborough was often quoted as saying, has 'a life to live as the greatest he'. But, paradoxically, amongst all the other social rights which were valued by working class people was the right to equality of opportunity in education for their children. They might want their children to maintain their loyalty to the collective solidarity of the older generation, but they also wanted them to have access to better jobs and a better material standard of life.

The position of immigrant workers as an 'underclass' in British society has to be understood against this background. They came from a variety of different positions in the class and ethnic system of empire. They included the rural and urban poor of the West Indian Islands; they included some West Indians who migrated because they were actually from higher class and status groups than the majority; there were Jat Sikh farmers amongst them asking to earn money to expand their landholding; there were poor peasants from Mirpur and Bangladesh; there were richer urban merchants from Bombay or Karachi; and there were the 'twice migrant' families who came to England after having gained middle class status either in business or in the lower grades of government service or the professionals in East Africa. Nevertheless, with a few exceptions amongst the merchants, they came from social positions which were, materially at least, far worse off than the social positions available in Britain. Not merely was it the case that Britain offered an opportunity to individuals to get on, but to acquire the rights of a British worker in the welfare state was to acquire an unmistakable position of privilege and security.

The problem of immigrant minorities in the fifties and the sixties therefore was whether they did gain the normal rights of employers or employees in the welfare state or whether they were excluded in their business activity in a separate social and economic pyramid and excluded as workers from participation in the normal benefits of the welfare state in such areas as employment, housing and education. My suggestion was that they were so excluded and that, as far as those who were workers rather than entrepreneurs and business men were concerned, this meant the creation of an underclass, a class, that is, of those who did not enjoy the benefits which were available to the incorporated working class.

There was, of course, never any formal and legal denial of rights to minorities. Unlike foreign workers in Europe who lacked nearly all rights in principle because they were not citizens, British immigrants had all the rights which flowed from citizenship. Moreover there never was the sort of educational situation which once existed in the Deep South of the United States where State Law denied to Blacks the right to enter certain state schools. What was the case however was that there developed de facto rather than de jure ways of denying Black and Asian workers their rights and that these were as effective in keeping them in an underclass position.

So far as employment is concerned the immigrant generation from Asia and the West Indies could obtain employment of some kind easiy enough. In fact what is surprising in the fifties is how little opposition there was to the simple fact of the employment of immigrants. This was because British born workers and their children were no longer willing to do a large range of unskilled and deskilled jobs, which were nonetheless essential if industry was to continue. What was the case, however, was that the jobs which immigrants did get were very largely confined to a few industries and to the least attractive jobs in those industries. Certain jobs it should be noted like mining, docking and certain sorts of constuction were actually not open to immigrants even though in countries like Switzerland and Belgium these were precisely the sorts of industries which did employ immigrants. This was because of trade union power which had turned jobs there into a hereditary property of communities and families. Jobs were easily available however in textiles, in the foundries, in public transport and in menial roles in the health service as well as in unskilled work in industrial manufacture. To a large extent regardless of education and skill Black and Asian workers were concentrated in these jobs.

By the late sixties it was apparent that workers in these situations lacked adequate trade union protection. Employers able to deal with all black shops or shifts tried to increase the rate of exploitation in these shops and shifts and they were resisted not by united trade union action, even though the workers were overwhelmingly members of the unions, but rather by spontaneous strikes by the immigrant workers themselves. In these strikes, moreover, the immigrant workers began to demand entry into the more skilled and better paid jobs and encountered the hostility and opposition of White British workers. Clearly there were signs of an incipient colour bar developing.

The marginal underclass status of immigrant workers is also shown by the statistics of unemployment. In times of prosperity immigrant unemployment was a transitory phenomenon largely occasioned by the problems of immigration itself. In 1960 it was still very high but by 1970 it was close to that of the population at large. What soon became evident with the recession, however, was that, as unemployment rose, it rose nearly twice as sharply amongst Black and Asian workers. Also, since much of the rising unemployment was concentrated on young people, to be young and Black was the least desirable fate of all. The fact of the matter was that when it came to it it was obvious that the assumptions of British immigration policy had not been very different from those which underlay the guest worker policy in Europe. Immigrant labour had been useful for a time but the society in general and employers in particular felt no great sense of obligation towards the children of immigrants or indeed to the adult immigrant unemployed.

For all that I have just said though, it could be argued that this does not add up to saying that immigrant workers constituted an underclass. The fact of the matter is that immigrant workers did join trade unions, and, given the influence of the large general and unskilled unions which they joined within the T.U.C. they were inevitably involved in mainstream class and labour politics and class and labour politics served their interests. But while there is truth in this, the kind of class solidarity which was generated was still limited. Class solidarity stopped at the factory gate. When the immigrant went home at nights, he went home to a largely segregated community and found that the power of the labour movement which was mobilised at the local level to provide working class housing was not mobilised on his behalf. He was left to do the best he could with the left over housing of the inner city.

In the immediate post war period there were two main ways in which British working class people sought to improve their housing conditions. If they had a sufficient and secure income they could obtain mortgage loans from building societies and buy good family housing usually in the suburbs. If, on the other hand, their wages were too low or uncertain, they could turn to the Council for good houses to rent. So far as this second option is concerned the great achievement of Britain is that it did provide for a third of its population good publicly owned rented housing without stigma. Very few countries in fact have a better record in this respect.

The existence of such options in the field of housing, however, had little meaning to Black and Asian workers in the fifties and early sixties. Estate agents, building societies and vendors were able to and did discriminate freely against Black and Asian applicants and house purchasers were forced to buy in restricted areas, and then with irregular forms of finance, while, so far as the rented Council sector was concerned, the points system was used to discriminate systematically if indirectly against Blacks. While it is true that both of these forms of discrimination were weakened after the passing of the 1969 Race Relations Act and with the abatement of the housing shortage in the public sector, the fact is that by that time many immigrants had been forced into making long-term housing commitments and quasi ghetto conditions had emerged. Moreover once this kind of segregation had started it perpetuated itself. New buyers chose to stay in the segregated areas because of the existence of communal facilities and because, in a hostile and racist world, they felt that they had protection there. Thus there grew up not merely a system of urban segregation but a situation in which the social bonds of a segregated residential community were at least as powerful as those engendered by working class membership. In Marxian terms, while the immigrant workers might have been members of the working class as a class-in-itself they did not share in the types of bonding and social consciousness which existed in the working class as a whole and formed if anything their own separate 'class-for-itself'.

The statistics of percentages of the population of wards 'living in households with a New Commonwealth or Pakistani head' (the surrogate statistic for the percentage of Blacks and Asians) shows that urban segregation is increasing. In Birmingham, for example, there are now 6 wards in which the proportion in NCWP households is 48% or more, the largest percentage being 71% (OPCS 1982). Below this there are a number of intermediate wards with between 20 and 40% but then, often in the wards next to those above 48%, the percentage drops to less than ten. The so-called Inner City wards have in fact become largely Black and Asian; some of the Outer City wards are as White as Torquay.

The segregation which has been imposed upon dark-skinned immigrant communities is reflected and amplified in the schools. The inhabitants of the

31

Inner City wards who are not Black or Asian are nearly all either retired people whose children and grandchildren have fled to the suburbs or Irish immigrants whose childrne attend Catholic Schools. The result of this is that nearly all the children attending the State schools in these wards are Black and Asian. In the Handsworth area of Birmingham for example all the Secondary Comprehensive schools have well over 90% of their children drawn from these groups.

What this degree of segregation in education means is not absolutely clear. We should clearly take seriously the opinion of the United States Supreme Court in the Brown versus the Board of Education judgement that education which is racially segregated is inherently unequal, but it has to be noted that, insofar as Black and Asian children have special problems, it is possible that they might be more seriously dealt with in Black and Asian schools than they can be in overwhelmingly White schools where the few Black children might well be placed in remedial classes. Moreover it is true that extra resources have been put into the school with high proportions of Black and Asian children. Unfortunately it is probably the case that both the minority in the White school and the majority in a segregated school get a bad deal. Strategies for dealing with the educational problems of these children are poorly developed and the process of segregation is not something which has been planned for the advantage of the students concerned. Rather the emergence of segregated schools as well as the appearance of Black and Asian minorities in White schools has been seen as an unfortunate accident threatening normal White education. This was the logic behind the now abandoned plans for bussing Black children.

Related to these three institutional forms of segregation and racial inequality is the question of how minority people and Black and Asian wards are policed and whether this is essentially different from the policing of other areas and particularly working class areas, for clearly the way in which the police act towards a group both reflects and determines the degree to which that group is accepted as a legitimate part of the society.

It is true, of course, that the extent to which the police behave with political impartiality in situations within White society, is a matter of debate. They have been thought to intervene against trades unionists in industrial disputes, to have restricted rights of political demonstrators, and, in dealing with young working-class crowds at football matches and musical festivals, to have behaved with 'brutality'. Nonetheless it is on the whole possible to argue about these matters in terms of some sort of shared consensus about the police holding the ring so that political and industrial processes can take their course, and the police are to some extent responsive to this debate. They are much less responsive to criticism of their policing of immigrant areas.

There are two somewhat opposite complaints made against the police by and on behalf of Black and Asian communities. The first which is common amongst Black youth is that they are 'harrassed'. The second more frequent amongst Asians is that they are not sufficiently protected against racial attacks whether by political or by criminal groups.

Clearly immigrant communities of Blacks and Asians have not been opposed to law and order as such. Like other people they look to the police to protect their lives and their property. This protection however does not imply in the case of Black communities, any more than it does in White, treating all those from the communities who appear in public as potential criminals. Insofar as this does happen whether under the old 'sus' laws or under 'stop and search' rules it clearly suggests that the police concerned are operating on assumptions other than those of maintaining law and order. In the experience of many Black youngsters, the police appear to act as though they were in a state of war with the community. That is how they see it in Brixton.

The other story about police behaviour is that of which Asian communities complain. Their houses, shops and temples have been daubed or made the subject of arson attacks; individuals have been physically attacked and sometimes murdered; and, at least in the seventies Neo-Fascist organisations like the National Front were allowed to organise provocative marches into their residential areas. Here the police are accused not of being over-zealous, but precisely the opposite. They are thought by their inactivity to have withdrawn protection from a section of the community and thereby left them open to attack.

It is in fact very difficult to discuss these issues openly because the police are well organised to defend themselves against criticism to a public which still see them as defending law and order in a valuable way. It is not, however, my purpose here to pronounce upon the validity of the criticisms. It suffices to note that there is a lack of confidence in the police amongst sizeable sections of the Black and Asian communities and that the enquiry by Lord Scarman suggested that in the case of the former at least there was much which had to be done to reform police practice before confidence could be won. From the point of view of this chapter what I want to note is that not merely are Black and Asian communities subject to unjust inequalities in the major institutions, but that their very right to be in Britain seems to be called into question by their experience of police behaviour. Such behaviour moreover reflects the implicit assumptions of our immigration laws which have been directed specifically at restricting Black and Asian immigration.

My conclusion then is that Black and Asian immigrants have during the fifties and sixties been not merely segregated but positively held down and oppressed in Britain. To say this, however, is by no means to say that this will be their permanent condition. The working class as such could be said to have been in a similar position in nineteenth century society and it has through class struggle and political action been able fundamentally to alter its position within the Welfare State. Surely then one might expect that the political action of the minority communities will make similar gains and that a new relationship between minorities and societies might be won as was the position of the working class in the welfare state.

That I think this will happen is implicit in the revision which I have suggested of Myrdal's concept of the underclass (Rex and Tomlinson 1979). I do not see the young Black and Asian descended communities born in Britain simply as some rotting and despairing mass. They have organised themselves, they have developed new forms of political consciousness and have found their ways of bringing pressure to bear on this society either directly or indirectly through the Labour movement. It is through this sort of action that I see a modification of the relationship of Black and Asian minorities with society occurring rather than through the paternalitic intervention of government. Indeed those very interventions, I will argue begin to change their nature as minorites begin to exercise real political pressure. Already local government behaviour was beginning to change before 1981 as more and more Councillors saw that they could only be elected with Black votes, but, after 1981 as the possibilities which were opened up by riots became evident, more and more local Councils came to accept the need for Equal Opportunty policies.

Before I turn to looking at the policy responses of government rather than the political action of the minorities themselves, there is one very important qualification which I must make about all that I have said. I have spoken about the incorporated working class in the Welfare State and have defined the deprivation of Black and Asian communities essentially as the denial of their right to share in Welfare State benefits. This, however, assumes that the consensus about the Welfare State which existed in the fifties and the sixties remains unchallenged. Clearly, however, it has been challenged from the right. What are the implications of this political change for Black and Asian minorities?

It seems to me that there are clearly two possibilities. The first is that insofar as the Welfare State is undermined or destroyed more and more native British workers will be in the position in which immigrant minorities have been all along. In this case a new and bitter class struggle which includes both native-born and immigrant workers will ensue and a new kind of integration will be available to minorities. This is something which I see as happening increasingly. Whatever its overt policies, the National Union of Public Employees when it strikes, strikes on behalf of that substantial proporiton of its lower paid members who are Black. So also in many other unions and one cannot begin to think of organising the unemployed without recognising that many of them are Black.

The other possibility, however, is that a process of scapegoating will be the predominant one. Instead of organising with the minority communities to fight against unemployment and for the restoration of the Welfare State it is possible that some workers will be persuaded that they should regain rights only for themslves and that this is best done by attacking the minority community. Speaking simply as a sociologist, I am surprised that this has not occurred to a greater extent than it has done. Speaking as a politically engaged citizen, I am delighted that it has not. But one should not let ones hopes and wishes stand in for facts. It remains quite possible that at some particular point during the developing economic crisis a political movement will be mobilised with an explicitly racist programme.

So far I have spoken of Black and Asian minorities as consisting of employed workers and their families. This leads to the view that their choice is between independent political action and action through the Labour Party. Now it is true that the vast majority of immigrants from both groups are in fact workers and their support for the Labour Party on class grounds has been reinforced by the fact that the history of anti-colonial struggle has led to a natural sympathy for labour in both groups and especially amongst Asians whatever their social class. What did happen in the 1983 General Election, however, is that an increasing minority of Asians and some West Indians voted Conservative. The Conservative Party Conference of 1983, moreover, supported the Asian and West Indian communities and their own members from these groups against a right wing racialist resolution. This might well be taken to mean that just as immigrant workers have gained some kind of acceptance in the Labour movement, so it has been accepted that the Asian business classes may look for a political home in the Conservative Party. This clearly represents an important type of integration in what remains a class divided society. Here again, however, we cannot assume that integration is complete or that racialism may not be revived. Quite possibly, after its defeat in the Conservative Party it may seek to organise outside and, if the growth of Powellism in the sixties is a relevant precedent such a movement may well flourish.

The theme of this chapter is that in the long run the only effective form of integration will be that which is won by the Black and Asian minorities themselves in the course of political struggle. Nonetheless no account of likely developments would be complete without some consideration of government policies, if only because in the long run these policies are influenced by minority political action.

34

Major policy developments in the sixties and early seventies turned on the concepts of disadvantage and deprivation. Since racial discrimination is always difficult to prove, those who wanted to see it rectified often chose, rather than accusing specific discriminators, merely to take rates of relative disadvantage as sufficient signs of discrimination. The notion of disadvantage, however, was a convenient one for those who did not wish to face up to the difficulties involved in combatting discrimination on a political level. They tended to represent it as a matter almost of accident and one which could be dealt with by compensatory expenditure.

Policy to deal with disadvantage was develped in relation to Educational Priority Areas and Schools, through the Urban Programme, through the Community Development Projects, through the Department of Health and Social Security's enquiries into Transmitted Deprivation and through the Inner City partnerships.

The only policy directed specifically to helping minorities rather than the disadvantaged as such was that embodied in the Local Government Act of 1966. Section 11 of that Act enabled government to give special aid to areas with high concentrations of immigrants. Even here, however, it should be noted that Section 11 is intended to give aid by helping areas rather than the groups in those areas. Other pieces of legislation involve rather more complex relationships between the needs of minorities and the needs of the disadvantaged Very strangely one of the criteria of educational disadvantage in the priority schools is that the schools have high proportions of immigrants, reflecting a common view that the presence of immigrant children is a problem to others, rather than suggesting that there is a section of the school population who need help themselves. Even more strange is the standpoint of the White Paper, Policy for the Inner Cities. Having argued that the decline of the Inner City is due to poverty, and having called for investment and job creation there to overcome that poverty, it then goes on to argue that many of the people of the Inner City are unsuitable for the industries to be reinvigorated and that they should move to the periphery. It would seem that here again it is the presence of minority people which constitutes the problem rather than the notion that they themselves have problems.

Policies based upon the concept of disadvantage suggested that, rather than adopting political strategies which would check or balance the power of particular groups and promote that of others, problems would be resolved through the expenditure of money. This was often represented as 'Positive Discrimination'. Unfortunately the effect of action of this kind was damaging in a threefold way. Firstly it had a labelling effect lumping all those with problems in a single category of the disadvantaged. Secondly it produced a backlash by suggesting that minorities already had their rights in a fair-minded society and were now being given more than their due share. Thirdly it involved the creation of a dual institutional apparatus through which the recipients of grants from the government became government agents and ceased to be politically effective on behalf of their constituents.

It is actually a striking fact that during the late sixties and early seventies it became a general policy to try to deal with apparently insoluble problems by giving money to those who raised them. Indeed the Community Development Teams had been created precisely in order to locate problems which could be resolved in this way. It might be said that such policies were doubly successful. They ensured that those who were a potential source of trouble were put on the pay-roll and thereby neutered and it also found a way of doing social work far more cheaply than through the orthodox channels.

This system was widely extended to ethnic minorities in the years that followed. The 1968 Race Relations Act created the Community Relations Councils which took probably several hundred potential political leaders out of the Asian and West Indian communities and set them to work for government. Then with a fairly small amount of money self-help schemes which were run by West Indian organisations for West Indian youth were given subsidies so that a still wider range of organisations were beholden to government, and, finally, as the control of the Urban Programme passed to the Urban Partnerships a substantial if not actually a proper proportional part of its funds were given to minority organisations.

I would be being altogether too dogmatic if I said that none of these programmes had benefitted Blacks and Asians in Britain and I would be unfair to the many vocationally committed people who work within them. I would insist, however, that on the whole the programmes which I have mentioned did very little to combat discrimination and that they undermined rather than supported the development of independent political action by people themselves. Much more important was the 'Enforcement' work begun by the Commission for Racial Equality after 1976 and continued as Local Authorities took up the task of creating conditions of Equal Opportunity for minorities.

The 1976 Act was actually a strong Act on the Enforcement side. It did provide for Investigations into Racial Discrimination; it did offer legal redress for those who suffered it; and it recognised indirect discrimination. All of these were strong positions and one which moved sharply away from the ideological notion that the problem was simply to deal with disadvantage. It is widely agreed, however, that the measures concerned were inadequately backed with resources of staff and money and still less by an effective political will to see them implemented. One question which was posed was whether it would not be more effective in combatting discrimination to lay emphasis upon administrative action rather than relying on the slow and uncertain procedures necessary for legal redress. To this end there were many who saw Section 71 of the Race Relations Act which called upon, even if it did not require, Local Authorities to promote Equality of Opportunity in their areas.

At first very few local Councils took any action under this section of the act at all, yet quite suddenly after 1981 numerous Councils began to take some kind of action. In fact a political will had been mobilised for the first time and it was widely agreed that this was the twofold result of the riots of 1981 and the ethnic minority vote. But, whatever the reasons, there had been a striking new development. The widespread nature of racial discrimination was recognised and it was this that the new Equal Opportunity policies sought to combat.

The actual policies being pursued by different local authorities have varied enormously, but a common programme which is developing is that of reviewing recruitment and promotion policies, monitoring the numbers of minority officers employed and educating those who have to do with selection or with dealing with members of ethnic minorities in what is called 'racial and ethnic awareness'.

The aspect of this policy which raises most doubt is that of training in racial and ethnic awareness. Very often such programmes rest upon the notion that what is required is simply attitude change and attitudes are seen in an idealistic way as having nothing to do with interests. It does seem likely, however, that even though he or she may go through racial and ethnic awareness training, someone who has interests which are served by racial inequality will at best only nominally comply with the attitudes which are expected of him, and at worst react against being preached at so that the programme is counter-productive. Against this it may be said that where there is a local authority which is in effect telling its members through laying on racial and ethnic awareness programmes that it is its policy to insist on racial equality, its employees interests will clearly lie in conforming.

What may be important about local authority policies on equal opportunity policies is that a certain momentum will build up behind them. So long as only the specialised officers of the Commission for Racial Equality preach the doctrine it is likely to have relatively little impact, particularly if the Commission receives only qualified backing from government. When, however, it becomes part of the ethos of local government to oppose racial inequality and when ordinary non-specialised officers accept this stand as part of their professionalism, something important has happened. Conceivably it might even have some educative effect on central government departments and on private firms.

To say that something is happening in local government which will help the move towards greater racial equality and integration is by no means to say that a new non-racial Utopia has been achieved. Nor is it to place great weight on native political parties at local level as agents of change. What we may be witnessing is some slight response to minority pressure, and if one holds as I do, that it is that pressure which can be the only ultimately reliable form of change, it would be foolish to ignore the responses which have now been wrung out of local government. Certainly, as one not given to optimism, I do see some change in the new policies as compared with those which focussed around the idea of correcting disadvantage.

In part independently of local authority equal opportunity policies, and in part as a result of them, another new development which has been strengthened in recent years is the idea of multi-cultural education. Unfortunately its relationship to equality of opportunity is often misunderstood. Thus for example a leading spokesperson of the I.L.E.A. when challenged with the idea that multi-cultural education would undermine levels of examination achievement was reported as replying that she was not concerned with the small elite who passed O and A levels but with the vast majority. Here multi-cultural education was seen as something to be contrasted wth exam success. What should surely follow from equal opportunity policy, however, is simply that no child should be debarred through his language and his cultural affiliation from attaining the highest levels of school success. Only within that should the question of providing this or that syllabus for those unlikely to succeed be considered. It is of the essence of the equality of opportunity policy that minorities should be found in appropriate proportions both among the successful and the non-successful.

One of the points which we continually have to bear in mind in all debates about segregation and integration or about assimilation versus cultural pluralism is that segregation and cultural pluralism can take two forms. On the one hand they can reflect the fact that within an overall situation of equal opportunity people choose to maintain different cultural, religious and domestic practices. On the other they can represent the provision for the minority of an inferior alternative. There clearly is a case for the kind of multi-cultural education which, while ensuring that individuals are not held back in a severely competitive and credentialling system, also ensures that minority cultures are fostered and respected at all levels including the highest. Such a conception contrasts sharply with what is often offered in the form of lessons on the steel-band for West Indian children and on rice-growing for the Asians while other children are doing real lessons. What has to be realised in general throughout society is that there is first of all equality of opportunity in the public domain and that, within that and secondarily, we go on to ensure that the creative and enriching features of a variety of communal cultures are fostered and sustained. I am not a romantic about this. I do not actually believe that all the cultures now represented amongst our minority populations will go on in their fullness forever. Even Asian cultures with their strong base in kinship and religion will gradually die away. What I do believe is that so long as people want them to exist in England they can do much to enrich the life of all of us.

One could envisage with hindsight the kinds of policies which central and local government might have adopted at the outset of Asian and West Indian migration to ensure the smoothest possible integration through the promotion of equality of opportunity and the recognition of cultural difference. Thus we could perhaps have had a peaceful integrated and unitary yet multi-cultural society. In fact things did not develop that way and we are having to pull ourselves up by our own moral and political bootstraps. There are points here and there within the total system where one can see the beginnings of the emergence of policies which might meet the needs of our Black and Asian minorities and preserve democratic values in our own society. If that policy is to succeed, and there is no certainty that it will, it is essential that it be adopted at the top of our political system and generalised throughout all institutions.

I would end by emphasising that one crucial sphere in which the twin ideals of equality and cultural pluralism has yet to be institutionalised is in the sphere of policing. It was perhaps surprising that when Lord Scarman was appointed to investigate policing methods in Brixton he was thought to be making a general study of race relations. That is almost the opposite of the truth. The understanding of the problems of policing multi-racial areas presupposes a general understanding of race relations and not vice versa. Yet it is true that how different groups are treated by those who in a democratic society have a monopoly of the use of physical coercion is central to what happens in race relations. If the police continue to hold archaic racist, conservative and colonialist values and bring those values to bear in the course of their policing duties, then any programme of equal opportunity and multi-culturalism is bound to fail. That is why the implementation of the minimal programme recommended by Scarman is so vital to any race relations policy. Unfortunately all that I see at the moment are small groups of serious and sensible policemen fighting to get a hearing.

This, however, repeats my general theme. The general political will for a just programme of minority integration has so far not been there and many of us have been able to do nothing but prophesy gloom and doom. What I am saying is that there is some small hope now that in response to the pressures which have come from the political action of our Asian and West Indian minorities themselves there has been some stirring of movement in a different direction. It remains to be seen whether it can possibly succeed. It will be a test of the strength of the democratic processes which can operate in our society whether it does or not.

IV   Race, law and politics

The study of law in abstraction from the social relations and the social system which it purports to regulate will always be arid and unreal. But sociology if it discusses only those aspects of social relations which are unaffected by legal sanctions is liable to be either Utopian or trivial. Nowhere is this more evident than in the discussion of the regulation of race relations by law. What we have to understand here is the interaction between law and political action.

It is interesting to note that when Clegg and Flanders published their authoritative System of Industrial Relations in Britain, (Clegg and Flanders, 1954), the lawyer whom they invited to contribute, Kahn-Freund, probably wrote the most truly sociological chapter in the book. Kahn-Freund saw that industrial relations in Great Britain were of interest to lawyers primarily by virtue of the fact that they were outside the law. As he put it, 'Reliance on legislation and legal sanctions for the enforcement of rights and duties between employers and employees may be a sympton of impending breakdown and, especially on the side of the unions, frequently a sign of weakness, certainly not a sign of strength.'

This remark has more than indirect relevance to our present topic, for, when Kahn-Freund and Wedderburn wrote an introductory note to Lester and Bindman's book, Race and Law (Lester and Bindman, 1972), they drew attention to the fact that a previous book in the same series, Hepple's Race, Jobs and the Law in Britain (Hepple, 1970), had seen the question of racial equality in the employment field far more as part of the system of industrial relations than as a matter of law.

At first sight this would seem to mean that industrial bargaining, class bargaining and action through the Labour party would be a better means of ensuring the rights of minority groups of workers than any reliance on legal right. Kahn-Freund and Wedderburn had both seen how attempts at the legal regulation of trades union activity could be damaging to the working class. Was it then the case that when James Callaghan took over the drafting of the Race Relations Act of 1968 and urged that industrial matters should be left in the first place at least to normal internal negotiating machinery, he was only extending this principle and allowing minorities to benefit from it? Clearly the race relations experts did not think so, for Callaghan was seen as inserting into race relations matters a set of procedures which not only would not guarantee justice to minorities in themselves but would prevent the operation of a legal process which could serve to do just that. The question then seemed to be sharply posed. Either we left these matters to the courts with all the dangers of a reactionary anti-working class and possibly racist bias on the part of the judiciary, or we saw this as a political matter, which, in Britain, meant a process of class negotiation.

For fear of being misunderstood, the position which will be taken at the end of this chapter should now be declared in advance. The choice is not the simple one just mentioned. Judges do tend to be biassed anti-working class and racist, but the trade union conscious working class is no universal guarantor of rights either; it exists to protect the rights and privilege of its own members and there is always the possibility that in entrusting race relations to the labour movement rather than the judges, one is simply turning for protection from one racist force to another. Obviously the answer must lie in another form of politics which enables the minorities member to confront the judges with his own advocate and the organised native working class with his own mobilised political power.

Those who were principally responsible for the creation of a legal machinery for dealing with race relations in Britain, of course, tended to draw upon American models. In doing so they underestimated the importance of three crucial differences between American and British experience. These were: firstly, the existence of a written constitution and a supreme court charged with implementing that constitution in the U.S.A.; secondly, the absence of class-based politics in the U.S.A. and the correlative increased importance of ethnic politics and the boss system; and finally the fact that Black Americans had organised politically for more than half a century to use both law and extra-legal power on their own behalf. Let us look briefly at each of these features of the American as contrasted with the British situation.

It is easy enough to represent the American legal system as dispensing only bourgeois justice. The constitution and the division of powers were dreamed up by substantial business men and the rights which they had it in mind to protect were their own rights against the unfair competition of their metropolitan equivalents and against the tyranny of the monarchy. And if, indeed, the constitution was devised by a coalition of bourgeoisie and slave-owning planters, in due time the former turned on the latter and after a bloody civil war ensured that it was bourgeois society which prevailed.

All this may be said, and there is no need here to rehearse the way in which the Courts extended the natural rights of property to permit the exploitation of child-labour. But that does not of itself make bourgeois law into racist law. Inherently the language of money knows no colour bars, and, given the peculiar history of the United States and the defeat of the plantocracy of the South by the Bourgeois North, the law was bound sooner or later to develop an explicitly anti-racist emphasis. When Black Americans began to organise to demand their rights through the courts they were doing the very thing that the courts were set up for, at least so long as they did not choose to fight their employers. True, the Plessey vs Ferguson judgement with its recognition of segregated facilities gave the South a breathing space, but in the long run the courts were unable and unwilling to allow even this. Black Americans like any others were entitled to bourgeois rights and, having established that much, were able to go on to claim other kinds of rights on which the Constitution originally had been silent or neutral.

The law, of course, was never unquestionably supreme. Both the personnel of the Supreme Court and the judgements which were tolerable or possible depended on the political state of play. But politics also had a distinct character in the U.S.A. They did not take the form of class politics, in which a coherent established native working class disputed ultimate control of the society with the bourgeoisie. Instead, the huddled masses of the largely Euroepan poor organised themselves in ethnic associations and sold their votes through ethnic bosses to the established parties in return for favours. Political power and ethnicity were deeply intertwined and being an immigrant or a minority member, so far from being a disturbance within an established political system, formed the very substance of that system. If the emancipated slaves of the South and the Black migrants to Northern cities did not immediately benefit from this system it was nonetheless a system geared to the fact of ethnicity and to ethnicity as a basis for the distribution of rights.

The potentiality of both this legal and this political system, however lay dormant so far as Blacks were concerned until they organised to take advantage of them. One line of thinking, of course, amongst Black political leaders, was to remain outside the system altogether, to choose secession or an African Zionism, and this is by no means an unimportant fact today in Britain as well as the United States. But there were also very American alternatives which could be pursued with the aim, not of getting out of the system, but of getting into it. A Black man could claim rights at law: he could assert his right to vote, he could share in the right of every American to carry a gun and in the ultimate right to revolution. The N.A.A.C.P. was the vehicle through which the full legal alternative was pursued. Employing the best available lawyers, including Black lawyers, and with the full anti-paternalist truculence which an adversary system of justice allowed, the N.A.A.C.P. campaign reached a kind of climax with the Brown vs the Board of Education decision, which opened a new era of social rights for the Black American. But insofar as law by itself could not be effective, Black politics of varying degrees of militancy eventually forced the President and the Congress to adopt programmes of Civil Rights, Affirmative Employment, Positive Discrimination, and more generally, anti-poverty programmes which, if they were effective, would benefit Blacks most because they formed such a large contingent of the poor.

The aim of what has been said above should not be misunderstood. It is not intended to whitewash the United States. White Power is still the basic fact about American society. Equality of opportunity has only been formally guaranteed, and has not led to equality of outcome. The process of desegregation has been slow and halting and for those who still live in the ghetto, the notion that there has been a Black revolution or that the Black American has at last been given a fair and equal place in American society is derisory. In fact it might be said that the main effect of the changes during the fifties and sixties, apart from the collapse of archaic Jim Crow practises in the South, has been the creation of a small Black middle class, and that even this is not a true middle class but a small group of beneficiaries of affirmative employment whom the society has found it convenient to buy off.

All of this may be true, but it is still the case that there are structural conditions which make against racial equality in Britain of a different kind from those which exist in the United States. Those with experience of the United States, particularly those with experience of the Civil Rights Movement there, too often talk as though the failure of Great Britain to achieve racial justice is similar in kind to the failure of U.S. civil rights programmes - that we have given our Asian and West Indian minorities equality of opportunity, but that we have failed to take the necessary affirmative action, failed to carry out programmes of positive discrimination and that it is because of this that deprivation and disadvantage, (two of our favourite words), still exist. What is to be suggested here is that we have not yet got to this stage. What we have is systematic old-fashioned negative discrimination and, so long as that exists, it is misleading and dangerous and damaging to minorities to engage in campaigns allegedly on their behalf calling for positive discrimination. Such campaigns are damaging because they suggest falsely that we have had some kind of civil rights programme, that West Indian and Asian citizens have equality of social rights and are now asking for more than their share. A good example of the kind of thing being referred to here was the 1965 White Paper on Immigration from the Commonwealth (Home Office 1965). The facts at that time, as now, were that West Indians and Asians were discriminated against in every sector of the housing allocation system. Instead of discussing this, however, the White Paper discussed whether there should be discrimination in favour of immigrants, (and incidentally decided against this, thus serving to confirm a false but widely held belief that 'immigrants', meaning West Indian and Asian descended citizens, were generally likely to get an unfair advantage in housing if the government did not interfere).

Lawyers with American experience who abstract the question of legal applications from an understanding of the sociological context can play a particularly misleading role in this matter. It is up to sociologists to remind them of the social context in which the law operates. In this case what has to be pointed out is that there is no written constitution or Supreme Court to defend it in Britain as there is in the United States: our political movements and parties have not arisen from ethnic associations of immigrants, but have been based upon class formations arising in the first place out of industrially based conflicts over wages and conditions. And there has not yet been that kind of political organisation and activity amongst minorities which confronts the courts, Parliament and the police with a real adversary. So far the debate has been conducted without either the constraint imposed by law or a political force arising from the action of oppressed and exploited minorities. The parties to it have been 'white liberals', (in the most pejorative sense of that term), who listen to what they regard as moderate and sensible minority opinion, and those who are explicitly against immigrants, the minorities or the blacks and regard their very presence in this country as illegitimate. In fact it is fair to say that no totally independent minority organisations have emerged. All of those which did come into existence were in some measure incorporated in government-sponsored activity and the record suggests that even then the only organisations which did ultimately survive were those which were fully under paternalistic government control.

In some ways the most independent organisation has been the Indian Workers Associations and there have been similar associations among other Asian ethnic communities. The I.W.A. has acted at local level to deal with Indian workers' problems, and has been active at the level of local Trades Councils. It has also attempted to exercise influence in local Council and Parliamentary elections in certain constituencies. It has, moreover, been a durable organisation quite unlike the relatively ephemeral organisations amongst West Indians. For all this, however, the I.W.A. is not yet an effective trade union or political party capable of mobilising Indian political power in a decisive way. It is as much India-oriented as British-oriented amd emphasises communal solidarity at the expense of purely instrumental goals. It is also prone to splits on issues which are of Indian rather than British significance, its leadership being divided between Communist, Maoist and Naxelite, and also between a separate communal organisation in the London borough of Southall and the national organisation.

West Indian organisations have been far less effective in bringing West Indian influence to bear on British politics. There clearly has not been any West Indian equivalent in Britain to the N.A.A.C.P. in the United States. True, there is reason for this in that the same clear forms of judicial redress were not available to British West Indians, but there has not been any organisation or set of organisations to which those who were victims of discrimination and harassment could appeal. The West Indian Standing Conference looked at one stage like being the principal organisation in this field, but it was always a federation of paper organisations and many of its leaders and potential leaders were creamed off into the Government's Community Relations apparatus. At the grass roots the organisations which dealt with people's problems tended to be as much Black Consciousness organisations concerned with the recovery of Black identity as they were actual political organisations. Even more clearly than in the Indian case they have directed their attention away from Britain which is conceived as Babylon, that is as a place of exile and captivity.

In the circumstances it is not surprising that any attempt at political, cultural, or intellectual organisation which was not directly part of the government apparatus tended to be drawn away from simple rational political activity either towards incorporation or towards some kind of external or secessionist goal. This can be seen in the case of C.A.R.D. (the Campaign against Racial Discrimination), the National Committee for Commonwealth Immigrants, and the Institute of Race Relations, each of which went through what could only be called a period of traumatic breakdown during the mid-sixties.

C.A.R.D. was formed at the suggestion of Martin Luther King as a British Civil Rights Movement. It is doubtful whether such an organisation was possible in Britain. King's Southern Christian Leadership Conference had succeeded in America in capitalising on the earlier work of the N.A.A.C.P. in the peculiar conditions of the Deep South. But it was challenged in the U.S.A. by both the surviving Garveyite secessionist tradition and the more militant Black Power theories. Inevitably, these tendencies had their overspill in the British situation at the time when C.A.R.D. was being formed. Malcom X visited Britain and encouraged Michael de Freitas, (later Michael X), to form the Racial Adjustment Action Society in 1965, and Stokely Carmichael was invited to England by the Universal Coloured People's Organisation in 1967.

It is true that neither the R.A.A.S. nor the U.C.P.O. had any lasting effect on minority politics in Britain, but their very existence served as a reminder that the relatively narrow and legalistic approach of a Civil Rights Movement would not receive an undivided response. But if such challenges from what some might consider the more militant side inhibited C.A.R.D.'s work, so also did the approach of those of its members who were pushing it in an even more orthodox and legalistic direction.

Necesarily, if C.A.R.D. was to work, it had to combine a capacity for mobilising members at the grass roots with a capacity to be politically effective in British terms. Antony Lester, Dipak Nandy and several others among the leadership of the organisation saw matters in this way. Their first goal was to get an effective Race Relations Act passed and they regarded C.A.R.D. as a likely base from which pressure could be exercised to attain this end. Unfortunately for them, the goal of getting a Race Relations Act passed was less important to some of the C.A.R.D. commttee than getting the organisation aligned with the Third World Revolution. They outvoted Lester and Nandy's group on the executive and proposed a series of militant resolutions including anti-Zionist ones which were bound to alienate part of the British liberal left. Lester, Nandy and others were forced to resign from C.A.R.D. and formed a new organisation, Equal Rights, to lobby for their bill. But this new organisation had no mass base and the two sides of C.A.R.D.'s 'personality' became split. The Equal Rights group, deprived of any mass following, came to look increasingly paternalist, while the briefly surviving C.A.R.D. leadership talked militantly but achieved little (Heineman 1972).

It should perhaps be noted that the Southall branch of the Indian Workers' Association participated in C.A.R.D. through its President, Vishnu Sharma, and that Sharma supported the Lester-Nandy group in the dispute. Subsequently Sharma became a full-time official of the Joint Council for the Welfare of Immigrants which dealt with matters of immigration rather than race relations and which, for that reason, was probably of greater importance to the Indian community. So long as a moderate version of C.A.R.D. existed, Indian leaders like Sharma were willing to support it, but they were unlikely to carry on such work on their own.

Tentatively, immigrant and minority organisations in C.A.R.D. had ventured to establish relations with radical or liberal British politics and had eventually abandoned the attempt. A similar attempt was now made by the other side, when the Government set up the National Committee for Commonwealth Immigrants. The attempt was equally unsuccessful. After a few brief years of existence, during which it showed some sign of providing the Government with a built-in political lobby on behalf of the immigrant communities, the N.C.C.I. was succeeded by the Community Relations Commission and its local Council, which had a quite different role.

When the then Archbishop of Canterbury was invited to assume the Chairmanship of the National Committee, he did seek the advice of immigrant leaders known to him before accepting; he did also say that, if investigations by the Committee suggested that immigration control was itself harmful to race relations, his Committee would be prepared to advise against the continuation of control. The Committee itself included David Pitt, a West Indian County Councillor who was probably the most significant West Indian figure in the Labour Party, and Homza Alvai, a leading Pakistani intellectual. Finally the Committee appointed a number of specialist panels to advise it on important aspects of discrimination. All these facts suggested a Committee which would be more than a mere goodwill organisation, and a possible spokesman in government circles for the political interests of the minorities. Almost immediately, however, this organisation, like C.A.R.D., began to be pulled apart by the strain towards militancy on the one hand and towards legalism and orthodoxy on the other.

If getting Pitt and Alavi to join the N.C.C.I. was a political gain for an organisation concerned to establish links with the immigrant communities, their decision to join it meant that both they and C.A.R.D. of which they were members lost the confidence of the grass roots. On the other hand, Michael Dummett who had been the prime mover in the formation of the Joint Council for the Welfare of Immigrants suggested that the N.C.C.I. should have gone wider and made itself virtually into a forum for immigrant and minority opinion. It is doubtful whether Dummett's solution could possibly have worked, of course, and it could be argued that he was urging an even more comprehensive incorporation of the immigrant leadership. But nonetheless it was clear that there was a wide range of opinion which regarded the N.C.C.I. as not radical enough.

Within the N.C.C.I. itself there were further divisions. The various panels put up their recommendations to the main Committee and called for radical intervention by Ministers, particularly in discrimination by local government. Proposals of this kind, however, were hardly listened to and it soon became apparent that, in the Committee itself, only two kinds of proposals were receiving attention. One was to enlarge the scope of race relations legislation and the other was to find non-political ways of improving community relations. Instead of continuing as a political organisation, the N.C.C.I. was pointing towards judicial solutions on the one hand and social work on the other.

The strongest tendency to emerge within the N.C.C.I. was the same as that which was emerging out of the ruins of C.A.R.D. which had virtually collapsed in confusion in December 1967. The lawyers who had lobbied for the first Race Relations Act passed by Soskice in 1965 were deeply dissatisfied with the compromise measure which he had introduced and had already persuaded the Home Secretary, Roy Jenkins, to introduce a revised and more powerful Act. The panels of the National Committee were thus used as part of a campaign to provide Jenkins with the necessary political ammunition to pass his bill. The final stage of this process was the setting up of two studies, one of the extent of discrimination carried out by P.E.P. (Daniel 1968) and one of the use of law to combat discrimination (Street 1967). There had been other research done and there was in fact plenty of justification for passing legislation, but the simple market-research type study carried out by Political and Economic Planning provided Jenkins with the kind of 'detached', 'objective' and 'scientific' evidence which clinched his case. The Act was already on the stocks at the time Jenkins left the Home Office for the Treasury and an important principle was established, namely that race relations legislation applied to the central spheres of employment and housing. The cost of this was that the N.C.C.I. in 1967 did little else but support legislation. The many political and administrative actions which could have been taken were abandoned.

But, if the N.C.C.I. had lost contact with the grass roots in the minority communities, it also began to lose the confidence of and to lose confidence in government. The new Home Secretary, James Callaghan, did not feel very strongly committed to race relations legislation at all, and accepted susbstantial modifications to the original draft. Crucially, witnesses could not be sub-peona'd and papers could not be called for the Board's investigations and the whole area of employment was closed to Board interference until industry's own internal machinery was exhausted. Callaghan thus trusted the destiny of the immigrant minorities to political rather than judicial powers, and the powers that mattered were essentially those of the Labour Movement.

Further than this, Archbishop Ramsey recalled his promise to intervene in matters relating to immigration control when, in February 1968, Callaghan introduced a quota system for British passport holders who were not patrials. The racist nature of this decision led the Archbishop to the view that it would be increasingly impossible for the Committee to continue its work. Callaghan accepted this and in his new Race Relations Act provided for the supercession of the N.C.C.I. by the new Community Relations Commission.

It will be useful here to summarise what, sociologically speaking, had happened in 1967 and early 1968. C.A.R.D., which itself did not fully reflect minority opinion but only that opinion which could contemplate working within a Civil Rights framework, had split between militants and legalists. Two members of C.A.R.D. joined the N.C.C.I. when it was set up and thereby lost the confidence of many active members of C.A.R.D. of all shades of opinion. The N.C.C.I. itself did not represent fully the opinion of its more radical members but served as a vehicle for the C.A.R.D. legalists' campaign for a new Act. Thus legal action came to take precedence over politics. But even this legal action was softened in its effect through the compromies which were made with political forces in mainstream politics. Unlike the situation in the United States where legal action followed political and where legal encounters took place on an adversary basis, here legal action was seen as an alternative to politics and the actual legal institutions were paternalistic in character.

If this were not enough, the new Community Relations Commission was to have a powerful effect on minority politics. The local liason committees which had been set up by the N.C.C.I. were now to be better financed and called Community Relations Councils. These Councils had to be staffed and once they were staffed the local staff had to be advised and organised by new staff at the centre. Some officers were appointed from the host community itself, but very quickly some hundreds of jobs came into existence for which men who might otherwise have been political leaders were admirably suited. Thus after it had been clearly demonstrated that Britain could not devise the institutional means through which independent minority members could become legislators, advocates and negotiators, the proposal now was that as many of them as possible should be taken on as employees.

What is being said here is not something simple like saying that the new C.R.C. staff had sold out. The fact was that there were simply no positions from which anyone who wanted to be a fully independent leader could act. Resources were made available on a new scale to the new officers and many of them, experienced as they were in the ways of the old colonial office, consciously set about being two-faced, taking the Queen's shilling on the one hand and winning benefits for their people on the other.

Closely related to these more overtly political developments were developments in the structure of the intellectual and research organisations through which Britain could begin to understand her relation with the minorities. The central role was played by the Institute of Race Relations, which interestingly went through its own trauma not unlike that of the N.C.C.I. and C.A.R.D. (Mullard 1985).

The Institute of Race Relations was an independent institution which emerged from an original period of tutelage in Chatham House. It was financed by grants from private capitalist industry and directed by Phillip Mason. For a long time it provided a forum for a wide range of opinion on race relations matters and was well known, particularly for its journal Race and to a lesser extent for the annual conferences which it promoted jointly with the British Sociological Association. In 1963 the Institute obtained a grant of £75,000 from the Nuffield Foundation and appointed E.J. Rose and Nicholas Deakin, the latter a close friend and ally of the Labour lawyer Antony Lester, to carry out a Survey of Race Relations in Britain, a task which was seen in the first place at least as equal to Myrdal's study of the race problem in the United States.

Colour and Citizenship, the report of the Survey of Race Relations, was published in February 1969 and a revised and abridged version by Nicholas Deakin the following year (Rose et al 1969, Deakin 1970). Both volumes, but the latter in particular, bear the marks of the times in which they were born. Deakin was very close to the legalists of C.A.R.D. and an admirer of Roy Jenkins. Thus the picture of the structure and dynamics of race relations which was emerging was exactly that which provided the intellectual basis for Lester's lobby for a new Race Relations Act. Meanwhile, a new and well-financed organisation, the Runnymede Trust, was founded with Dipak Nandy, another associate of Lester's, as its first director. The Runnymede Trust became the institutionalised voice of liberalism on the race question.

It was natural that Deakin and Nandy should serve on the Board of the Institute of Race Relations as it laid plans for its new research. Together with other well-known liberals like Sir Edward Boyle, academics like W.G. Runciman and representatives of the Labour party like Joan Lestor, they seemed to guarantee its objectivity and intellectual respectability despite its known financial backing.

At the very moment that the Institute's research work was coming to fruition, however, it began to run into difficulties. The Social Science Research Council rejected an application for a grant of £90,000 for a second survey conducted by the Institute and decided instead to create a Research Unit in a University setting. The Institute then got its finance from the Ford Foundation and launched two research programmes, one a domestic programme which was located in the significantly named Joint Unit for Minority and Policy Research at Sussex and directed by Nicholas Deakin, and the other an International programme directed by Hugh Tinker and located in the Institute itself. The trouble for the Institute arose because of the kind of polarisation which we have been discussing all along, which now showed itself in the Institute's work. The Sussex Unit obviously and avowedly addressed itself to policy rather than political problems, while the Overseas programme quickly moved towards radicalism.

The key figures in the trauma which followed were Robin Jenkins and the institute's librarian, A. Sivanandan. Jenkins presented an interesting and provocative paper entitled The Manufacture of Knowledge in the Institute of Race Relations (Jenkins 1968) to the race relations group of the British Sociological Association and some members of the Board called on Tinker to dismiss him. Tinker resisted and did so again when the Board took exception to the mild radicalisation which the popular journal, Race Today, underwent under the editorshp of Alexander Kirby. The Board decided to send Tinker, who had by then become Mason's successor as Director, on study leave for the remainder of his contract.

At this stage Sivanandan used his inside knowledge effectively to oppose the Board. Proxy votes on which the Board had previously relied for its re-election were obtained from a wide range of members and the Board's decision on Tinker was rescinded. The majority of Board members resigned, leaving behind a group of Black radicals and a handful of academics including Louis Kushnick, Lee Bridges, Robert Moore and John Rex. After a few months, however, the new Board decided that it had no use for academia and accepted a number of resignations including my own. Subsequently, the respected journal Race had its name changed to Race and Class and attempted to follow an editorial line combining Marxism and Black Militancy. The popular journal Race Today became even more markedly radical and was eventually run by a group of young West Indian intellectuals who became known as the Race Today Collective.

This incursion into the history of the Institute and of social research into race relations generally may appear to be irrelevant to a paper directed to the topic of Race, Politics and Law. But essentially the problem facing the Institute was the same as that which had faced the N.C.C.I. and C.A.R.D. Like them, it provided a kind of forum in which political views could be developed and pressure brought, albeit by intellectual means, on the government and policy makers. It could have been the sort of body whose influence could have been used to make the law work in a non-paternalistic way. This may well be what Sivanandan and his colleagues feel they have achieved. The alternative assessment is that the body has quite different goals, too radical to be contained within formal British politics and, for the moment, more concerned with mobilising the exploited minorities than with achieving particular political objectives. If this assessment is correct, then, with the other part of the institute's heritage being used to solve problems for policy makers rather than bringing political pressure to bear on them, the break-up of the Institute merely reflects the more widespread failure of British society to provide the institutional framework within which political and legal action can be used together to overcome racial injustice.

It remains to be seen whether any other centre can develop which provided knowledge and intellectual resources which can be effectively used by minority people in their fight for justice. The question is whether there is a position between policy-orientation and a militancy irrelevant to British politics. In theory it seems possible that a University might provide a setting for work of this kind. But, if recent experience is anything to go by, universities have tended to produce research which is politically irrelevant or, in the wake of 1968, new kinds of dogmatism. There does not seem to be any kind of institutional guarantee of preserving the kind of centre I have been describing. Anyone who takes on such a task has to live by his wits, recognising that in the last analysis even the protection of an academic institution cannot defend research and political thinking from forces which affect the larger society.

If the story of the sixties is one of splits, of traumas and collapse of the institutions through which race relations were mediated, this does not mean that at the end Britain was left without race relations institutions. The one institution which survived and which came to have a near monopoly of its field was the Commission for Racial Equality. It is in many ways the inevitable product of the sixties, and brings together both the culmination of the legalistic approach and the kind of paternalism which was unavoidable once C.A.R.D., the N.C.C.I. and other bodies had been cleared out of the way.

Looked at as a purely legal institution, the new Commission seems at first sight to have much to be said for it. The Commission has powers to carry out investigations into industrial firms, housing agencies and other organisations if there is a prima facie case that its policies are producing racial disadvantage. Given the necessary staff, moreover, it would seem that, with power to call for documents and subpoena witnesses, the Commission will be able to obtain information of a kind never before available, and to use this information as a basis for issuing non-discrimination notices. But at the very time that it has been given powers to act abrasively and aggressively in order to set new standards of racial equality, the Commission has also been asked to undertake not merely the task of the old Race Relations Board but also that of the old Community Relations Commission and to promote good community relations.

A case can be put, and is put, that the positive community relations side of the Commission's work provides an essential background to its work for racial justice. It is, however, a very dubious case. Minority organisations are not yet well enough organised to act in the Courts and in politics as the N.A.A.C.P. did in the U.S.A. Until they are, it is advantageous that there is a body which can act as their advocate. But no-one would accept as an advocate in a court of law someone who was known not merely to be inclined but to have a duty towards winning the goodwill of the other side. It seems inevitable, therefore, that the investigations into discrimination will be held back and inhibited by fear that the host community and, more particularly, British politicians, will take offence. That is why one hears it said within the Commission that if the powers of investigation were used to the full, Parliament would very quickly remove them.

There is, however, an even worse feature of the present situation from a minority point of view. This is that the Commission is not merely performing a holding operation until the minorities are able to speak and act for themselves in the courts and in politics. At this stage it would seem that the Commission's very existence stands in the way of the emergence of independent spokesmen. Not only are considerable numbers of potential minority leaders the employees of the Commission, but the Commission in 1979 also disposed of a budget of some half a million pounds for self-help projects carried out by community groups. Thus, far beyond the range of its own staff, the Commission will exercise control over the budgets and therefore the actions of community groups.

The same budgets which tempt Black community leaders also tempt sociologists. It seems likely that there will emerge in Britain a new industry of race relations sociologists and lawyers who will work within the system and also work the system. They will do so in the name of action research, of praxis and more loosely of getting something done. So be it. I would only conclude by saying that there are two other things a sociologist might do. He might be concerned to describe the structures which exist as they are and predict likely outcomes in a non-Utopian way. Or he might look at the size of the problem facing the minorities in trying to move from a situation of effective paternalistic social control to one of hard-won justice, and recommend to them what has to be done. To recommend these tasks is to risk alienating many of those working in the race business with a furious moral zeal. But they are tasks which must be performed if we are to have honest academic sociology, or, one supposes, honest academic law.

Two factors have subsequently played a part in the development of British race relations. These are the urban disturbances or "riots" which occurred in 1980, 81 and 85 and the growing effectiveness in inner city constituencies of the Black and Asian vote. It is too early to judge what the long term effect of these developments will be, but it would seem likely that they will do somethng to displace purely paternalistic initiatives and make the achievement of minority rights much more likely.

V Old and new themes in urban redevelopment

Social change and social reform in Britain in the brave new world of 1945 was directed by values derived from the fact that we live in a society in which the formal rationality of industrial capitalism had been challenged by the substantive rationality of those who knew where the shoe pinches, the working classes, whose political party had imposed on the system the new ideals of Fabianism. For a while at least, in the early fifties, this meant that there was an interparty consensus around the ideas of the Welfare State, Full Employment and the Mixed Economy. Those ideas were spelled out in terms of a system of social insurance, a National Health Service open to all, equality of opportunity in education, and a measure of planning in the economy as a whole. The same values were implicit in housing and in urban affairs and a concept of urban development arose in which the slums of the inner city would disappear and be replaced by suburbs and New Towns, in which families, secure in their properties or tenancies, would attain the full dignity of social citizenship.

Let me in no way underrate the importance of what was achieved by post-war governments in these spheres. It so happens that by marriage I have become a member by affiliation of one of the most encapsulated working class communities in Britain in the Yorkshire coalfields. There, a powerful trade union and a permanent Labour majority have won for the people a security of employment, a dignity and a social security which they never had before the war. It is expressed in a thousand different ways, but above all it is expressed in Council Housing, which provides, at a low rent, housing of a material standard far higher than that which is available to the working classes in most industrial countries.

Yet, with this said, it has also become abundantly clear that the housing and planning policies through which this housing standard was achieved are in many respects grossly insensitive to the realities even of core working class life. This was something which I was to learn as my colleagues and I addressed ourselves to the problems of mining villages during my stay in the University of Durham.

In 1945 the planners and Labour Councillors envisaged a new urban world whose contours were so clearly depicted in the little blue Pelican books of the time. Le Corbusier once said that the duty of the architect was not necessarily to reflect a way of life but to propose one. What the new planners proposed was their own version of the vision of Le Corbusier combined perhaps with the Garden City ideal of Ebenezer Howard. But, whereas Howard, certainly, and possibly Le Corbusier, had wider social ideals, what issued in the plans was simply a notion of better individual houses, built in tidy places with reasonable access to the countryside, or more commonly, in the great industrial centres, tower blocks, saving enough space on the ground for the introduction of a bit of greenery.

For a long while, while these plans still awaited implementation, the miners and their families accepted them. They trusted their Councillors to work out in architectural terms a way of life which expressed their own strong feelings of community. But when the plans began to bite in the early sixties, they discovered that their own villages were often listed as 'Category D', as being unsuitable for future maintenance, and that they were to be assigned to tidier larger towns of about ten to twenty thousand people. They looked at their existing communities with their five or six hundred people, their pubs, their chapels, their overlapping social ties and the familiar fields and streams which surrounded them, and they saw nothing in the planned alternative which had anything to commend it. Somehow the ideals of 1945 had taken a bureaucratic and administrative form, in which they were the units of administration. They knew, and we as sociologists were to discover, that the things which men lived for went beyond a high standard of individual housing. The Government then responded by appointing the Skeffington Committee on participation in planning, but when Mr Skeffington visited Bishop Auckland he was pelted with old fashioned political eggs.

The point which I am making here, however, is not simply a political one. The fact is, that, important though the research on housing standards was that had been conducted in terms of a bureaucratic discipline of social administration, the sociological knowledge necessary for its implementation was negligible. Sidney Webb, the founder of Social Administration had, it is true, in his original Fabian essay (Webb 1889), derided individualism and called for a collectivist approach to the provision of social services, but it was a collectivist approach in which an elite of administrators administered the people as so many units. It was this approach which began to run into crisis as the social plans of the Welfare State came to be implemented.

These observations might, of course, be dismissed as somewhat romantic. After all, it can be said, we no longer live in the folksy communal world of the original Durham miner's villages. We live in a large scale society, most workers live in large connurbations, and effective social provision had to be provided on a bureaucratic basis. Labour Councillors, moreover, representative as they are of the working classes, approved the system and wanted to achieve the hard-headed practical goal of decent housing standards for each individual family.
It was precisely their achievement in this respect, however, which I had come to question in the research which I had done in Sparkbrook, Birmingham before I went to Durham and which I continued after my return to the Midlands in 1970. It became increasingly clear to me that, although the Councillors and planners were committed to and would achieve much with regard to the improved housing of a privileged section of the working class, they were not coping with the problems of many other categories of people, and that the sociological dynamics of urban change were something that they had hardly begun to understand.

When Robert Moore and I went to Sparkbrook in 1963 (Rex and Moore 1963), we did so with many strong Fabian Socialist prejudices. Housing inadequacy and the problems to which it gave rise were essentially problems which arose from uncontrolled capitalism. It seemed to us that what we needed was more public provision of good rented housing which would prevent the working man from being at the mercy of the private landlord. British political traditions, we believed, would prevent the city from facing the sort of outcome which had been so graphically described by Park and Burgess in Chicago in the twenties (Park and Burgess 1925), where, as they saw it, in their Social Darwinist way, the basic urban process was competition for land use. The task of social policy here must therefore be to protect the tenant against his landlord so long as he was a private tenant, but, in the long run to move him to the kind of standards and security which Council owned rented housing could provide.

There is, of course, something to be said for these convictions as a basis for the long-term planning of housing, but, if even the first stage of a slum-clearance programme and the rehousing plans which followed it were to take twenty years, there was a considerable problem for those, whoever they were and for whatever reason, who stood at the back of the queue. It was not sufficient simply to punish those who provided for these people at standards well below those of the working class Council House ideal. The reality of life for a good long time for most people was the reality of the so-called twilight zones, and, however much we might tell them that in the long run they would be provided for, they would reply with justice 'in the long run we are all dead'.

As we saw it, bureaucratic socialist provision of housing did not entirely eliminate privilege within the system of housing allocation. Private enterprise, even with the aid of the credit of the bulding societies provided only for the economically secure and the well off, those who had power in the housing market. But, with Council Housing by no means available to all the remainder, political power in the housing allocation system produced graduated life-chances for men in cities, as surely as did market power, when the whole question of housing was left to private enterprise.

I was led to suggest as a theoretical formulation of the problem that just as on a more general level, capitalism produced class struggle, and that the struggle of the subordinate classes led to the acquisition of minimum rights which the system would not of itself have conceded, so in the housing sphere those who lacked access to housing opportunities would form housing classes and that the underprivileged would struggle as classes against the privileged. Urban politics, indeed, I saw as almost primarily a class struggle over housing opportunity, although one in which two privileged classes exercised power, and the underprivileged had not yet developed the political means for exercising their power except in a defensive way.

The privileged classes, of course, included, apart from those who could pay their way in the private market, those who already had Council tenancies and those to whom the allocative system would guarantee such tenancies in the forseeable future. Since, however, this latter group meant locally born working class families, there were many others who were either not locally born or did not have family life of a normal approved form. These others had to take what part of the housing stock remained and develop their own system for its allocation amongst themselves.

After the slums awaiting demolition in the fifties and the privately owned and single-family occupied housing in the inner city had been taken out, the main form of housing available consisted of large and formerly grand terrace houses not suitable for single family occupation. These could be bought and occupied by many amongst the underprivileged who had the necessary commercial sense, if they were prepared to balance their books by letting rooms. In so doing, of course, they provided rooves over the heads of all the other groups who were left out of the housing allocation system.

To put this in more specific terms, we found that in Sparkbrook Pakistani immigrants, of whom a few might have been business men but most were peasants, bought up the big houses with the aid of five-year bank loans supplemented by loans from friends and relatives, housed their incoming friends and relatives free, and let off the remaining rooms to West Indian and Irish families and to British people with social problems of all sorts.

We attained some unpopularity with our friends and some unwanted popularity with others, because we suggested that these landlords were as much sinned against as sinning. For those who administered the local housing system, whether councillors or local government officials, these landlords were the worst type of irresponsible capitalist, lowering housing standards, exploiting their tenants, and creating in their houses a hells brew of social and personal problems. We argued that these landlords were necessary by the default of the local authorities, were themselves an exploited housing class, and provided a service for other classes even less powerful in the total housing system than themselves.

Our instincts still led us to believe that the way in which people in a ward such as this would resolve thier problems was through the local Labour Party. But very quickly we found that the party surgery held in the Labour Club, which was a part-British part Irish Working men's club, was primarily concerned with considering and processing the housing claims of the native-born and Irish workers and their families. Many others, however, native as well as immigrant, found increasingly that their needs were only likely to be considered by their own social organisations working through a new community association which had come into being. The surgeries of the latter were far more radical places than those of the Labour Party. They were not simply concerned with the mediation of privilege, but with the human problems facing all of the population.

Of course men were not solely organised in classes or interest groups. What Marxists call classes-for-themselves require organisation, common ideas and a common sense of identity. But such bonds as these are unlikely to be established on a class basis if men are bound together by the strong ties of kinship and ethnicity. Thus the class-like formations through which men pursued their interests were usually ethnic associations which served both to advance those interests and to provide the social framework within which they conducted their lives. Although the lodging-house areas could never be single race ghettoes, almost by definition, one saw emerging ethnic sub-cultures and communities of a fairly lasting kind which were going to make Birmingham a multi-racial city. This kind of social formation was hardly understood in British sociology, and still less in the science of social administration, which governed the thinking of those in the Town Hall (Rex 1973).

The problem people who were housed with and through the immigrants in the early sixties did become an object of concern for the science of social administration. A series of reports began to draw attention to the condition of the new urban disadvantaged poor. Educational Priority areas were established, there were the new Urban Programme, the Community Development Projects, the D.H.S.S. investigations into transmitted deprivation and, not least in their final impact, the Inner City Studies. Characteristically all of these programmes based themselves on the attempt to find some kind of common index of individual attributes which could be used as a basis for administering a mass of individuals. The idea that these were groups of people, with active ongoing social relations capable of acting on their own behalf, if they found the means of political organisation, was foreign to the administrators. Characteristically, when the Department of Education and Science was called upon to create a centre for studying immigrant educational problems, it established instead a Centre for

Educational Disadvantage, which, according to the Minister of the day, would also be a means of dealing with immigrant problems.

Our study of Sparkbrook, then, attempted to bring to light some of the social problems of the lodging house zone as it existed in the early sixties. It did so, by using, not the normal statistical techniques through which British social science contributes to social reform, but through a combination of policy studies, small-scale in-depth surveys, studying institutions at work, and, I suppose, of participant observation. We certainly felt that our work owed more in its inspiration to Ernest Burgess and William Foote Whyte than it did to the heirs of Sidney Webb. In the long run its impact was to lie more in the mobilisation of new political forces and in improving the knowledge and practice of grass roots local government officials and social workers than it was in providing the administrators with scientific proofs. Above all, we felt that, instead of working within the framework of normal routine social science, we have opened up new problems and broken new ground.

In subsequent research with other colleagues I have found it necessary and much more rewarding not to address myself to the problems which governments and local authorities have posed in the spheres of housing policy and race relations. I find that as a general rule it is always wise to treat government itself as the problem rather than the people it administers. In the short run this always means that one is denounced as irresponsible and controversial. In the long run I think that the kind of Civil Service which we have in Britain is capable of taking on board, if only slowly and reluctantly, the conclusions of unorthodox investigations which raise problems which their routine enquiries would not have brought to light.

In the sphere of housing and minority group relations history did not stop at the point at which we concluded our investigations in Sparkbrook. On the one hand, official policy making had to be directed to the question of what to do with the next worst housing after the existing slum-clearance programme came to an end. On the other hand we knew that the local authority had been encouraging immigrant applicants for Council houses to leave the list and buy up this next worst housing with the aid of Council mortgages. The more the problem of housing immigrant families loomed, the more official discourse about the problem became deracialised. What we were told was a problem, was a problem purely of housing policy. But there was some substantial evidence both at local authority level and at the level of government that a very large consideration in the making of housing policy was that of finding an alternative medium term solution for housing immigrants so as to prevent a racist outcry if they began to appear in suburban estates.

The smaller privately owned terraces which became designated as General Improvement Areas and later as Housing Action Areas were also the terraces into which coloured immigrant families moved as their families were completed by immigration. Some did so because discrimination prevented their getting mortgages elsewhere. And some moved in as tenants of the Housing Associations, which took advantage of the improvement policy to convert old houses and let them on a less discriminatory basis than the Council did in relation to its own houses. Later, it is true, the Councils discriminated less as the housing shortage became less severe, but by then many of the immigrants had made more permanent arrangements and were disqualified for rehousing.

When I returned with my colleague, Sally Tomlinson, to research in Birmingham, it was in the Soho and Handsworth wards that the most crucial developments in housing were taking place (Rex and Tomlinson 1979). Both areas had been largely designated as General Improvement and Housing Action areas. In the former areas a decision had been taken that all houses in the area were eligible for improvement grants. In the latter, a house by house survey was being made as a result of which some houses would be demolished and replaced while others would be improved. Much research was being directed to the working out of these housing and environmental problems, including action research associated with Housing Advice Centres. The problem of Handsworth was being defined in a deracialised way as essentially an environmental problem. Although the area was in the secondary ring and actually close to Birmingham's border with Sandwell it was being increasingly referred to as an archetypical Inner City area.

I shall return later to the origins and significance of the whole Inner City problematic. As we saw the problem which was perplexing Birmingham, however, this was pre-eminently a multi-racial area. It was conceived as a problem not simply because the housing stock was deteriorating - the deterioration was no greater and no less than in other areas and no-one had actually shown that improvement was not actually occurring in a physical sense - but, given the fact that immigrants were channelled into the area in the fifties and sixties, and that, after the late sixties it was actually one of the lowest areas for inward immigration in Birmingham, the population was increasingly West Indian and Asian. We decided that the focus of our concern should be on the formation of ethnic sub-communities and the interaction between them.

By the time of the 1961 census these two wards were recognised as the main centre of West Indian, particularly Jamaican, settlement in Birmingham. Although the West Indian population was only about 11% and the total of West Indian and Asian immigrants about 13%, Handsworth was generally regarded as the main West Indian centre of population outside London and certainly enjoyed a reputation of being a developing centre of West Indian culture. By 1971, however, the overall pattern had changed. Soho ward had an immigrant population of about 29% of whom the majority were Asian, and Handsworth a population of about 20% evenly divided between the two groups. When British born children of these populations were included, 49% of the population of Soho were descended from New Commonwealth parents and about 35% of the population of Handsworth. In the National Dwellings and Household survey conducted by the O.P.C.S. in 1978 the percentages regarded by interviewers as of Asian or West Indian parentage were 66% for Soho and 50% for Handsworth, with about four fifths of the immigrant population of Soho being Asian and about half each being of West Indian and Asian ancestry in Handsworth. A majority of the White population in 1971 were actually over 60. By the time of the 1981 Census the percentage of Blacks and Asians in Soho was 71% and in Handsworth 57%.

The change which had overcome the two wards was not, in fact primarily one of housing and environmental deterioration. What had happened was a cultural transformation of the area. Instead of being an area of housing for semi-skilled and skilled manual and clerical workers from the White population, which had been the characteristic feature of the area in the interwar period it was an area housing three very different and not very compatible populations.

The Asian population was the newest and, in Soho ward at least, by 1978 the largest. Being relatively new, the adult population at least spoke limited English. Hindu and Sikh temples were established and tight familial control of children and young people prevented very much in the way of intermixing. The great propensity of this population for shopkeeping, as well as the need to supply the goods which would make the maintenance of the culture possible, meant that many of the main shopping streets took on a new and very Asian appearance.

The adult generation of West Indian workers had by the late seventies been in Handsworth for periods of up to twenty five years. They were settled in their houses and many had been in the same usually unskilled jobs for ten years or more. This generation was overwhelmingly conservative in its social customs, and contained a high proportion of churchgoers, including a significant minority who were members of the Pentecostal churches. The younger generation were not, however, tightly bound to their parents as the Asian children were and many of them were very responsive to new cultural forces related to the notion of Black Consciousness, especially as expressed in the Rastafarian religion and culture. Overt racism by Whites, discrimination and poor employment prospects for youth served to reinforce the teaching that the West Indian people had been four hundred years in slavery in 'Babylon', and that the reassertion of a Black Identity should be their prime concern. Even young men with no religious inclination quickly picked up these ideas from the lyrics of reggae songs and affected the Dreadlocks and the hats of Rastafarianism. Some few were in conflict with the forces of law and order and police suspicion of all young men wearing the rasta symbols on the street led to regular confrontations on the streets and in the police stations. These conflicts led to the area being regarded by the Whites as a dangerous area and an area of potential riots. To a smaller extent the Asian population feared these new tendencies, although most Asians were themselves sufficiently aware of the fact of racism to have some sympathy with the West Indians.

White flight had occurred to a very considerable extent. Whereas the vast majority of Asian and West Indian adults were in the economically active age groups and had young school-going children, the Whites were predominantly retired people. The fact that they stayed in the area despite the cultural transformation was a sign of the strength of their ties with it. One by no means has to suggest that they were racist to note that they felt a deep sense of resentment that the Council had assigned this particular destiny to the part of Birmingham that they regarded as home.

One particular transformation which stood out was that in the schools. With the White child population having virtually reached vanishing point the schools were overwhelmingly 'coloured'. In the main comprehensive schools in the area, the percentage is well above 95% and the child in Handsworth or Soho inevitably goes to a school where the largest element in the school population is Asian with the West indian population a little smaller. The schools benefit from positive discrimination but the actual educational enterprise which is conducted within them is an unknown quantity. The teachers are still overwhelmingly White and have little training, whatever their degree of sympathy and skill, for coping with the problems presented by different groups of Asian and West Indian children.

Whether in education, housing or any other area of policy, those who administered the services as well as those who did research on their operation, were disinclined to treat the problems which were evident as inter-ethnic or racial in character. There was little place for such conceptions in official discourse. Nonetheless the area was obviously a source of problems and, since these problems were rarely, if ever, attributed to the discrimination which had selected the population, the problem was seen in traditional social science terms as an environmental and economic one. The groundwork was laid for the emergence in public consciousness of the Problem of the Inner City.

The title of this Chapter is <u>Old and New Themes in Urban Development</u> and I have been describing some of the new themes which I came to think important in my researches in Birmingham. It is not simply that I was preoccupied with questions of race relations. The fact of the matter was that one could not really begin to understand what were being perceived as urban and environmental deterioration unless one understood the processes of racial discrimination and segregation which were going on. This, however, did not prevent most of those engaged in research from continuing to talk about the old themes, to address purely housing and environmental questions or, at best, to look at the social and political issues in purely traditional terms, that is, in terms of an improvement in the conditions of the native-born and established White working class.

There is, of course, a value consensus informing most urban research in Britain. It is not simply that we treat as objectively necessary that which is in the interests of the bourgeoisie or of capitalism. That may well be true in some countries, but a century of working class struggle and the growth of administrative Fabianism have made it untrue here. The need for public control and intervention to provide employment and housing for the working classes are part of received doctrine. What is not often realised, however, is that the new and morally comfortable consensus all too often ignores the interests of those at the bottom of the scale who are not fully protected by the trades unions and the Labour Party. This was one of our major discoveries in Sparkbrook. There the Labour Party did all that it could to improve the housing situation of the White workers by getting them into Council houses, but saw the lodging houses, which were actually providing accommodation for immigrants, simply as an evil to be suppressed. Moreover, when it came to declaring areas for redevelopment, it was the little redbrick cottages occupied by long-established British and Irish families which were chosen, while the larger terraces where the lodging houses were were simply passed by.

To emphasise my point further: when we originally raised the question of discrimination in housing policy which funnelled the immigrant workers, first into the lodging houses, and then into the improvement areas, we made reference to the political difficulties facing the politicians in the City Hall. We said, 'We know that your electors would resist the appearance of immigrants on Council Estates, but you would be wrong to take what appears to be an easy way out. In the long run, you will face both racial and environmental problems of a far worse kind in the twilight zones and the Inner City and these problems will be of your own making'.

If, however, we saw racial discrimination as leading to an intensification of environmental problems, the opposite conclusion was being drawn in the Higher Civil Service and amongst liberal minded Labour politicians. The political cost of making special provision for immigrants or of even pursuing a policy of justice towards minorities was too high. It was therefore suggested that what was wanted was an environmental policy, or at least a policy within the consensus about housing provision, in the hope that this might be an indirect way of helping minorities. The term 'low profile' was increasingly used in this connection, as in a number of other areas of social policy, where government departments insisted that they were not doing anything special for immigrants but would benefit them indirectly as part of the deprived, the disadvantaged and the Inner City poor. My own answer to these approaches was to say (a) that there was no answer available along the lines suggested since improvements along traditional lines would only reinforce existing inequalities (b) that I was not advocating what was called 'positive discrimination' which would give an unfair advantage to minorities and be politically unacceptable but (c) that I was advocating the ending of old-fashioned negative discrimination against the immigrants which was the prime cause of the problems under discussion.

Turning to the issues raised by the Inner City policy itself, it is to be noted first that the concept began to be used after the Long Hot Summer of 1967 when the

United States cities were burning. Previously, as, for instance in the deliberations of the National Committee for Commonwealth Immigrants we had used such terms as Areas of Special Housing Need and the like, but when we used the term Inner City, we were taking over an implicit analysis of the developing situation which came from the United States.

No-one who has known the United States in the full span of years since 1945 can but be struck by the change which has come over the major cities. Even up till the mid-fifties cities like New York and Chicago were regarded as exciting cosmopolitan places to visit and to live in, and the urban sociology of that time reflects that fact, along with the existence of deviance of all sorts in the 'zone of transition'. But, after about 1965, urban sociology describes cities as being in financial crisis, as being subject to uncontrolled and accelerating deterioration, and even as being places of terror. The middle classes and the Whites flee the central city, and a goodly ring beyond, leaving the public school system and the streets at night to the Blacks. There is a desert of abandoned sites and buildings, which looks like a bomb-site achieved without bombing, and the only hope of change in such areas is that building speculators might somewhat arbitarily single out a particular area for what they now call, using the British term, 'gentrification'. Ironically these sites cannot be used for building public low-cost housing for the poor because the law says that such housing should not be provided in racially segregated areas.

This image of the Inner City problem derived from the United States was very much in the mind of those who conceived of the Inner City studies in Lambeth, Birmingham Small Heath and Liverpool 8 in the early seventies. The aim was to see whether there were environmental policies which could arrest the process of urban decay, save the Inner City areas and make the city as a whole a safe place to live in. Incidentally the policy was thought of as a race relations policy, as a means of improving the conditions of the immigrant minorities, but quite often this was confused with an opposite notion, namely that of saving the city from the minorities.

Considerable confusion surrounded the publication of the Government's White Paper (Department of the Environment 1977a). It came clearly enough from the Department of the Environment and it began by saying that it was not concerned with the question of racial discrimination which it saw as a problem for the Home Office and the Commission for Racial Equality. Nonetheless it was widely discussed as though it was an answer to race relations problems, and the Minister himself, during the Labour Party's party political broadcast attacking the National Front, said that the policy was the Party's way of fighting the National Front.

In fact what strikes one about the White Paper is that, while it is innovative in going beyond the bounds of normal departmental thinking, its innovation lies in taking account of the needs especially of the native working class. It is very much a document written within the two party consensus of the Welfare State. The trouble is that it is supposed to be dealing with the problems precisely of those who are not covered by this consensus.

The main innovative points of the White Paper are that it establishes the link between employment on the one hand and housing and environmental problems on the other and that it proposes Partnerships between central government and designated local authorities, which will not only put central government clout behind ailing local policies, but will also bring employment and planning policies to bear in a way which is not normally open to the local authorities. These innovations have won much support for the policy in Socialist and Labour circles, where the belief has always been held that environmental and housing problems are ultimately of subordinate importance to those of employment, and where central government intervention has always been favoured. My own more cynical comment would be that possibly the government has now moved to a style of political and administrative thinking which just catches up with the problems of the depressed areas of the thirties, but which has not begun to comprehend the new problems of the Inner City of the seventies. In other words what we are talking about is a policy worked out in terms of the existing consensus and designed to satisfy the interests of those who are parties to that consensus.

Within the framework of the new administration what is proposed is basically a transfer of industrial and housing resources from the New Towns of the future. With relatively limited resources however, the most that can be hoped is a rather second hand New Town in which the patching of houses in the General Improvement Areas is accelerated, and new factories are sited in amongst these improved houses.

Perhaps the most startling and unexpected part of the Inner City Policy, however, is that which refers to population movement. The kind of industry which is envisaged for the area is one which will require more skilled labour than was the case in the dark satanic mills of the old industrial city. In these circumstances the existing residents might well be unsuited to the kinds of jobs available. Many of them, the White Paper says, are unskilled, semi-skilled and retired and they might do well to move to the periphery. They would then be replaced by a more suitable labour force who would come back to the improved housing which was being provided.

In speaking of the United States I said that one thing which could happen was that certain inner city areas might be gentrified, that is taken over by the middle classes. In Britain this is less likely to occur outside of the metropolis. But just as the suburban move to semi-detached housing was a publicly sponsored as well as a private phenomenon, so what one might see in Britain is a publicly sponsored process of gentrification, or, more exactly, the reconquest of the Inner City by the native working classes. It is hard to believe that the tide of anti-immigrant feeling in the country which has influenced so many other policies since 1945 has not had influence here. However deracialised the public discourse might be, there is often a shared and unspoken assumption that it is the immigrants in the Inner City who are the real problem. The solution to the Inner City problem therefore involves getting rid of the immigrants. It is not actually suggested that they should be expelled from the country, but they are directed vaguely to 'the periphery' at a very time when resources are being transferred from the periphery to the centre.

The future for the immigrant minorities under the new policy looks to be bleak. Of course, since, contrary to popular belief, neither the first generation immigrants nor their children have some hereditary trait which makes them unskilled and semi-skilled by nature, many of them will compete for the new jobs and try to stay. But the improvement and housing action policy might very well prevent that and they may find themselves either confined to the tattier parts of the housing stock interspersed amongst the new factories or simply forced to move.

Much will depend on the actual local government officers who implement the Inner City Policy as to how it works out. My own impression is that the younger generation amongst them, far from being in any sense racist, are more intelligent and better read men than their predecessors. Yet the strictly non-racist policies which they implement derive from the two party consensus and inevitably work to the advantage of some groups and against others. For a long time, for example, improvement grants were confined to houses of below a certain rateable value, but since these were the small houses occupied by single and usually White families, they brought no benefit at all to the minority families still living in single family occupation. The replacement of privately owned houses by houses converted into Council flats to let also biassed the system against those for whom house ownership was a preferred pattern. And, finally, often with the best of liberal intentions, the planners set out to get a 'better racial mix' even if this meant reducing the percentage of a particular racial or ethnic group and breaking up existing communities.

I notice that when Inner City Policy is being discussed and particularly when ethnic minorities' rights are at issue, what most people talk about is not the main structure of the Inner City Programme which absorbs about 90% of its resources and energy, but the old Urban Programme, for which the Partnerships have assumed responsibility, and which accounts for the other 10%. This is a supplementary policy for the poor who fall by the wayside rather than a main part of social planning. All too often, when one raises the question of minority rights, it is assumed that one is talking about the share which they receive of this charity. It might be added that there is a legitimate argument even about this share, but that should not direct the argument away from the thrust of the Main Programme.

My aim in this chapter, however, is not simply to enter into political argument about the inner city policy. It is to reinforce the point that bureaucratised social science operating within a consensus which arises as a resultant from working class and other pressures within the welfare state closes off consideration of new problem areas. Urban policy is still governed by the need to satisfy well organised political interests. The social scientist might well therefore see his role as one opening up new problems for discussion which, while central to urban policy, do not occur to those who think solely within the consensus.

The problem to which the research which my colleagues and I have drawn attention is that of the absorption of minorities, and not only ethnic minorities, into the urban system. This is not a problem which is central to present thinking because that thinking is based essentially on the preservation of the priveleged rights of those classes which are capable of exercising political power. From that standpoint there is no solution of minority problems beyond a vain hope that the minorities will disappear.

From my perspective, one of the first tasks of Inner City Policy should be precisely the task which the Department of Environment's White Paper rejects as not being its responsibility, namely that of overcoming discrimination. Without a policy on this matter, the graded distribution of social rights within the Welfare State will always leave out a substantial minority of the population who will constitute some kind of underclass, whose very existence will be perceived as a problem.

This set of problems will not be solved, moreover, through a policy of forced assimilation and dispersal. Just as the study of housing policy for the working classes from the Bethnal Green study onwards came to recognise that working class communities should not be ruthlessly broken up to satisfy administrative convenience, so also in the case of minority communities, there are communal ties of great social value whose preservation will bring great benefit to society as a whole.

To some extent this will mean commitment to the notion of a multi-ethnic, multi-cultural city rather than the creation of a single grey and uniform suburban way of life. But it need by no means imply the creation of purpose-built ghettoes. If the minority communities are given the opportunity of easy entry into the main society, many of the younger generation will become fully absorbed of their own free will, while others will move towards a more relaxed and possibly suburban ethnicity, which is already a quite well-known phenomenon amongst the descendants of Jewish immigrants both here and in the United States. In the meanwhile an urban system needs to provide for a period of about fifty years for the protective bonds which the minorities have created for themselves within the inner city. This will mean the creation of ethnic communities to the cultural enrichment of the city as a whole. And for the non-immigrant minorities the Inner City might also become the site of specialised social services geared to the meeting of their needs. Merely providing more jobs on the doorstep and improving the quality of the physical environment will do little to solve these problems.

Here, then, is a new task to which the tools of social science can be applied. It by no means implies that social science should abandon its commitment to rational and even to quantitative techniques. All that cannot be accepted is the absorption of the social scientist into the bureaucracy, measuring the attributes of individuals, and processing them so that they must either pass into the established and privileged class system or rejected as an underclass. If, however, this is what happens, the social scientist in a free society would be as justifed in putting himself at the service of the underclass in fighting for their rights, as he would serving the government and the consensus as a tame technician.

VI   Race and the urban system

Any serious attempt to understand the interface between urban sociology and the sociology of race relations and racial conflict must begin with the work of the Chicago school. Unfortunately, however, the meaning of this propositon is too often misunderstood. The significance of the Chicago school has come to be seen in terms of later insular, national American preoccupations, both methodological and political.   On the methodological front, these preoccupations have been directed to the improvement of quantitative measurement to the virtual exclusion of any sustained interest in community, class and ethnic relations, while on the political front they have been concerned with the measurement of segregation as it has presented itself as a political problem within the American political system (Lieberson, 1963, 1969; Taeuber and Taeuber, 1965).

In fact, the work of Park and Burgess raised questions of far more general significance.   They were concerned with the question of the incorporation of immigrants into an urban industrial society; they were specifically challenged by the migration of American Blacks from the semi-colonial system of the Deep South into urban and industrial life; and they saw that the master processes which determined the relations between 'host' and immigrant communities lay not in simple cultural differences but in the politico-economic sphere, specifically in the process of competition for land use. These topics must still lie at the centre of serious urban sociology, not merely in the United States, which is something of a special case, being largely an immigrant society and one in which relatively unrestrained capitalism determines the allocation of money, land and other resources, but also in other advanced industrial societies in Europe and elsewhere, where immigration to the cities encounters a long established native-born community, where a part of that immigration is from countries even more clearly colonial than the American deep South, and where the political action of the native working class has had the effect of restraining, to a degree, the operation of free capitalism in the allocation of resources.

In the period immediately after 1945, the expansion of the capitalist economies of North Western Europe called for an additional supply of labour. Since the rising aspirations of the peoples of North Western Europe precluded the possibility of an adequate supply of labour from native sources either in the continuing backward

62

parts of industry or in the most advanced industrial, areas where a process of deskilling (Braverman, 1974) was increasingly evident, this expansion of European economies demanded the recruitment of labour from countries where workers could be found who would work willingly in the unwanted jobs. Germany sought to fill the gap by recruiting so-called 'guest-workers' from Yugoslavia and Turkey; France drew on the populations of the relatively backward countries on her Southern border, as well as on North Africa and the more remote overseas departments of the French community; Switzerland built upon the long-established institution of seasonal labour drawn from Italy and Spain to recruit a more permanent labour force from these countries; Britain drew upon the vast resources of labour in the Indian sub-continent and on the stagnant economies of her own Deep South in the Caribbean; Sweden drew upon the overflow of guest workers from Germany, engaged in her own Southern recruiting, and continued as always to employ workers from her more industrially backward neighbour Finland; and the Benelux countries each worked out their own mix of immigrant labour drawn both from Southern Europe and from their own and other countries' colonies (Castles and Kosack, 1973). Although the percentage of immigrant workers in the total workforce remained small, certain sectors to industry came to be overwhelmingly dependent upon immigrant labour, and in some urban wards, in a limited number of industrial centres, the immigrant workers were in the majority, and hence the immigrant labour question moved to the top of the political agenda.

The need for replacement labour (Peach, 1968) was so manifest that, so long as the new workers were not in competition for the more wanted skilled and protected jobs, industrial conflict in the workplace between the organisations of native-born workers and their unions and the new immigrant workers was more limited than might have been expected. Conflict did occur, however, on a more generalised level over demands in all countries for a restriction of immigration as such, and on a more specific level over housing and other social welfare benefits. The conflict, therefore, appeared above all as a conflict within the urban system.

An adequate comparative study of the place of immigrant workers and their descendants in European cities has still to be carried out. Some crucial questions, however, may be posed as a result of studies conducted in Britain during the period between 1960 and 1980 (Rex and Moore, 1967; Rex and Tomlinson, 1979). They are of interest since they provide an enrichment of urban theories derived from American experience. In contrast to the United States, British urban policy has been profoundly modified by the restraining element of working class political power at the national and local level, and by the development of partially socialist approaches to housing. While this certainly does not mean that all the problems of urban segregation and conflict have been solved - indeed the thesis of this chapter is almost the opposite - it does mean that the attribution of these problems to the operation of unrestrained capitalism may well be called into question.
A number of recent commentators (e.g. Lipset, 1969; Bell, 1962; Marshall, 1977) have suggested that we now live in a post-capitalist society marked by a consensus around certain policies such as the maintenance of full employment, a mixed economy and the welfare state. These ideas are acceptable enough, provided that it is recognised that any such consensus rests upon the existence of working class power which is its guarantee and that it would be precarious in the event of the kind of defeat of the working class which is evident in Britain in the eighties. So long as the consensus lasts, it would seem that the process of urban management involves considerable interference with the free market and that housing above all becomes a matter of social provision.

Any European visitor to the United States would notice that the question of working-class housing appears there to be primarily a question of the operation of the free market. Low-cost rented housing is provided only for a small minority who are regarded as requiring special provision and the acceptance of such housing is seen as carrying with it a stigma. Similarly publicly provided free health care is confined to a tiny minority of the specially unfortunate. In Europe by contrast, and above all in Britain, subsidised rented housing has been provided for a large part of the working class - in Britain about a third of the total population - and has not been thought of as carrying a stigma. Similarly, the aim in health care has been the provision of a universal free service paid for largely out of general taxation. Only with the decline of working class power has it been possible for parties of the right to restore a two-tier system, in which those who can afford to take care of themselves do so in a free market, while the remainder of the population - still a majority of the working classes - use the subsidised free services.

All of this has had its effect on urban dynamics. Park and Burgess envisaged an urban process which could be likened to a continuous game of leapfrog. There was an initial urban core divided betwee the rich and the powerful, the middle classes and the workers. Very quickly, however, the rich abandoned their central urban residences to move to the better suburbs and, following them, the middle classes moved further out to the suburbs. The workers remained where they were unless, sharing in the increasing prosperity available to the majority in an expanding industrial society, they too joined the middle classes in a suburban migration. The vacated houses and their sites in the centre were then likely to be made over for business uses, but, until they were, they provided living space for incoming workers, particularly in the form of multiple-occupied lodging houses. By 1922, therefore, it was possible to see Chicago as having four urban residential zones outside the central business district and the industrial zone running from the centre to the periphery. These were the Zone of Transition, where the incoming workers lived, the Zone of Working Men's Homes, the Middle Class Zone and the Commuters' Zone.

No doubt it would be possible to bring Park and Burgess up-to-date by looking at subsequent moves in the game of leapfrog. The rich and powerful will often have left the city altogether, moving with the aid of improved private and public transport beyond the suburban periphery; the old workmen's homes would have been abandoned to more established immigrants as more and more workers have moved to the suburbs; the inner city will have continued to decay with sites and buildings being abandoned as they ceased to produce sufficient rents, unless they happened to be chosen by speculators for 'gentrification', that is to say for modification or rebuilding in the form of high cost apartments for the new urban middle classes; and, finally, the mostly Black poor will be fending for themselves as best they can, in a situation in which low cost rented housing is restricted, because it cannot legally be provided in segregated areas, and in which various restrictions on the free market by private individuals prevent their buying into the suburbs. Some such model would fit Chicago even today.

Initially, major British provincial cities underwent a process of development very similar to that described by Park and Burgess. The rich and powerful built their original homes on desirable sites near the centre; speculative builders provided terraces of small redbrick houses for the workers on the least favoured sites in the eighteen forties and fifties; and, towards the end of the century, larger terraces were built for the aristocracy of labour and for the increasing number of white collar workers. In due course, the rich moved to new mansions in the suburbs and with the expansion of credit facilities, particularly through the building society movement, large numbers of white collar people were able to move to the suburbs to semi-detached homes bought with mortgage loans.

What was different in the British situation began to occur at the very time when

Park and Burgess were writing, that is, just after the First World War. The wartime government of Lloyd George had promised the troops "homes fit for heroes to live in" and their Labour successors began the business of building so-called Council houses at subsidised rents on a massive scale. Particularly when Labour was in power in local City Councils, there began to emerge, alongside the semi-detached suburbias of the middle classes, new public suburbias of Council houses. They could not, of course, be built simply anywhere. The high cost of land prevented that and even today successive Labour governments have failed to find any way of reducing land costs through such means as the nationalisation of development value. They were also restricted in standards because of interest rates on money borrowed, interest rates which were never brought fully under public control. There was, however, sufficient leeway in the system to make a considerable advance possible and for the mass of the established working class to envisage the possibility, during their family-raising years, of renting, with considerable security of tenure, a good three-bedroomed semi-detached suburban house. Such housing became one of the desired ideals of the working class and the possibility of obtaining it came to be thought of as more important than any other service and as the very raison d'etre of Labour Power and the Welfare State. It was also, it should be noted a considerable political achievement. No housing of the same quality if provided by private enterprise for the working classes in other countries. And it is important that no stigma attaches to it.

In addition to this publicly-sponsored suburban migration, Labour power was exercised to legislate against the private enterprise system in many other ways and the civil servants in the successive ministries, responsible for housing, came to accept many ideas for housing reform sponsored by the Labour Party, or by its intellectual arm, the Fabian Society. Rents were increasingly subject to control and the private tenant protected against arbitrary eviction. Planning controls were exercised over the use of land and buildings, and the rights of landlords, particularly of multiple-occupied buildings, were restricted. Powers of compulsory purchase were exercised over the now slum houses, built in the eighteen forties and fifties, and in the immediate post war period, vast areas in the major cities passed into public ownership. In Birmingham, for example, the City Council controlled some 50,000 such houses awaiting demolition and temporarily housing less fortunate working class families.

All of this meant that the British city in the nineteen sixties had a shape and a character significantly different from that described by Park and Burgess for Chicago in the twenties. Middle class housing, it is true, was often poorer in standard than its American equivalent. But years of Labour-inspired reform had produced an entirely new pattern of working class rented housing. If one looked for zones equivalent to those described by Park and Burgess (Rex and Moore, 1967), one would have to list, apart from expensive middle class housing in the better suburbs and beyond the periphery, and semi-detached commuter homes, the huge new Council estates, the inner area slums awaiting demolition, but under Council control, and, to some extent, new inner-city Council estates often including ambiguously valued high-rise tower blocks. Apart from these, there remained a declining number of privately owned or rented houses fairly near to the city centre still occupied by ageing middle and working class families, and other larger houses for which neither the rich, nor the middle classes, nor the established working classes had much use.

With all this said, however, we now have to notice that conditions of scarcity prevailed and that they prevailed not only in the private sector but in the public or 'socialist' sector. All except the very worst housing was affected by this scarcity and, the better the housing, the less freely it was available. If the free market provided for those best able to pay, therefore, the City Councils had to find some system of choosing between the larger numbers of potential tenants who had some political claim to its houses. Hence the 'list' and the 'points system' which became crucial in the allocation of housing rights.

In explaining the housing system of the British city in the sixties, my colleagues and I found it useful to employ the notion of 'housing class'. Taking from Weber (1968:927) the notion that class situations arose wherever there were markets arising from differential control of resources, we went on to suggest that such differential control existed in relation to the means of housing as well as the means of production, that differential control existed in the bureaucratic sector of allocation as well as in the market, and that men formed associations and groups to defend their interests in this sphere, just as they did in the labour market. We suggested, therefore, that, in the contemporary British industrial city, one might expect to find class-like formations based upon (1) the outright ownership of whole houses, (2) ownership of desirable houses with the aid of mortgages, (3) ownership of less desirable houses for purposes of single family occupation, (4) rent-paying tenancies of houses listed under (2) and (3), (5) rent-paying tenancies of 'Council houses' on the more desirable estates, (6) rent-paying tenancies of Council houses in rebuilt inner city areas, (7) rent-paying tenancies of Council owned houses scheduled as slums and awaiting demolition, (8) ownership of large old inner-city housing on terms which necessarily required the letting of rooms to tenants, (9) tenancies within houses of type (8) (Rex and Moore, 1967).

What came to be called the 'theory of housing classes' broke new ground in several respects. It suggested that the separate sub-communities in the city which Burgess had noted were not merely culturally different but had a base in what might be termed economic or material interests. It argued that these classes or interest groups formed one of the main bases of urban politics. It claimed that 'housing classes' were to some extent distinct from industrial classes, though obviously they overlapped with them. And, finally and radically, it argued that the simplistic categories of ownership and tenancy did not reveal the most crucial distinctions in the city, since classes arising under the conditions mentioned under (8) and (9) above were the most underprivileged in the urban system, whereas classes arising under the conditions listed under (5) and (6) were relatively privileged.

A mass of individuals sharing a common position in the housing system, however, is simply a category, or as Marxists would say, a class-in-itself. To become a true class or a class-for-itself the individuals involved would have to become conscious of their common interest and organise to fight to defend it. Such developments rarely occurred on a self-conscious rational basis, however, unless those who shared the same housing position were already bound together by other bonds such as those which existed amongst ethnic immigrant groups. Ethnic bonds were important, therefore, but not solely because of their cultural significance. Rather, they had a role to play in subjective class formation.

To be more empirically specific about this, what we found in the City of Birmingham was a situation in which the established working classes had fairly considerable power within the total housing system, which ensured that sooner or later the vast majority of their members would be housed with secure tenancies in desirable Council houses, that is to say that they would have access to the publicly organised process of suburban migration, but that these rights would not necessarily be accorded to immigrant groups, or, indeed, to other categories of individuals whose way of life did not conform to that of the established working class. This was achieved through a points system according to which families were accorded points depending upon such factors as length of residence, standards of housekeeping and so on. The rationale of the system was that long-established working class people would resent the settlement of newcomers and deviants on their estates and that there would, therefore, be intolerable conflicts there. Unfortunately the solution proposed also had its costs. It meant the creation of inner-city areas which would themsleves be seen' as danger points for the system as a whole.

There is, of course, no reason why social structures of the kind which we found in Birmingham should be universal. Obviously, their specific character turns upon the peculiarities of British political history. What is true, however, is that all urban systems have a housing stock of differing degrees of desirability, that the allocation of houses within this system depends upon market power and political power, and that the action of the excluders and the excluded depends upon particular cultural and political factors of some kind. On this basis we may indeed risk the generalisation that the history of urban systems is always a history of housing class struggle of some kind.

Even our own subsequent empirical researches in Birmingham showed that it was necessary to modify our theory somewhat. We found that, although West Indian immigrant families to some extent approximated to British cultural norms and sought tenancies of publicly provided housing, Asian immigrants had little interest either in rented housing or, in many cases, in suburbanisation if it meant the breaking up of the ethnic community (Dhaya, 1973). It was, therefore, necessary to recognise differences in the position of frustrated potential Council tenants, frustrated house owners, and those who had so little attachment to the going value system that they chose a different housing style, even if, within that style, they did not get all that they wanted. Secondly, we saw that the lodging house phenomenon was, within the British context, only a temporary or partial expedient and that, as time went on, other alternatives would be opened up for single family occupation by immigrant families. These other alternatives included especially the development of a system of loans for house purchase by the City Councils designed to help families, not eligible for Council tenancies, to buy older inner-city properties and for the conversion of old houses into properly designed flats for rent by housing associations (Karn, 1978). Thirdly, we came to see that, although those in the least desirable housing situations were not simply the working classes or the poor, it was nonetheless the case that those who were in these housing situations were more or less those who occupied inferior positions in terms of conditions and negotiating power at work (Rex and Tomlinson, 1979).

These variations, as time went on in the British situation, however, represented the natural way in which the British system, with its particular mix of private and public provision, would react to the problems presented by underprivileged minorities who were not part of the constituency of working class representatives on the City Council. In the American situation, and in some European contexts, the working out of new policies for the underprivileged might have been left to speculators working on a private enterprise basis. In the British case, it was the Councils and central government which acted to make what was thought to be appropriate provision. At a later stage still, as we shall see, Central and Local Government combined to deal with the problems which the new inner-city housing system had created, with a Policy for the Inner Cities (Department of the Environment, 1977b).

Prior to 1967 the approach of Central Government to the development of housing in cities had been based upon the concept of redevelopment. That is to say large areas occupied by slum property were gradually cleared and the sites assigned, if not immediately used, for housing or industrial development. But, as the major slum-clearance programmes came to an end, a decision had to be taken as to whether the next worse houses should be scheduled for demolition, or whether they could be kept in reasonable condition by a policy of private and public improvement. A widely used concept in the housing literature was that of the 'twilight zone', implying that it was possible to hold back the night of approaching slumdom by catching and saving these houses in their twilight phase.

The decision which was taken (Department of the Environment, 1968) was that there should not be further massive slum clearance programmes, but that owners of houses in 'improvement areas' should be given a massive subsidy to improve their houses, particularly by installing basic amenities such as bathrooms and running water where these did not already exist, provided that the owners themsleves made a small contribution to the cost. Subsequently, improvement areas were supplemented by 'housing action areas' within which local government inspectors would visit all the houses in an area and decide for each house whether it should be demolished with minimum compensatiom to the owner and replaced by a Council-owned house, or whether it should become the subject of an improvement grant.

What is striking about all this when it is compared with similar developments in the United States, is the scope and scale of government intervention. It may be said that, without formally abolishing private ownership in inner-city housing, central and local government had assumed wide-ranging responsibilities for its management. Coupled with the wide-ranging powers over these areas arising from town planning provisions, these new management powers make it clear that there could not be the kind of blight due to site and building abandonment which one sees in cities like Chicago today.

With this said, however, it must again be pointed out that public intervention in housing management by no means implies substantive rationality based upon some conception of universal justice. The system which we have just described is precisely an alternative system to that which is involved in the normal provision for working class housing. Moreover, within this alternative system, there is considerable opportunity for discrimination, not merely between one house and another, but between one tenant and another.

It will now be useful to stop for a moment and recall the two successive housing systems which have evolved to meet the needs of those who slip through the net of the normal housing system. The first is that which is evolved by private enterprise when there is no clear public provision. The second is that which emerges as the public authorities intervene.

In the first system it must be understood that what emerges is not a ghetto. Statistical indices of segregation show that the lodging house zone is far from completely segregated on an ethnic basis. But, if the dynamics of the lodging house system are understood, it clearly cannot be. What happens is that there is a considerable range of individuals who are left out of the normal system. Amongst these there are some who have sufficient initiative to set about housing themselves in conditions of severe constraint. What they wish to do is to provide housing for themselves and their kinsmen at the lowest possible cost, and, to do this, they have to let off rooms to anyone prepared to pay a high enough rent to balance the nearly rent-free tenancies of friends and relatives. In the case which we studied, the initiative in setting up the lodging houses was taken by Pakistani and Bangladeshi settlers, many of whom were peasants. Amongst their tenants, however, there were the families of West Indian and Irish workers, Irish itinerants (the so-called tinkers), broken and single parent families, discharged prisoners and mental patients and any other category of individuals who were excluded from normal housing (Rex and Moore, 1967).

A housing system of this kind inevitably led to racial conflict. Such conflict occurred between tenant and landlord, but this was more limited than might be expected, since the tenant saw no alternative to his present landlord, and sometimes expressed appreciation for the accommodation provided when the normal housing system failed. Much more evident, however, was the conflict between the lodging house population as a whole, including landlords and tenants, and two kinds of neighbours. On the one hand, there were the older, respectable owners and tenants of inner-city houses who blamed the coming of the immigrants for the deteriorating and alien quality of their neighbourhood. On the other, there were the relatively underprivileged tenants of the Council-owned slums, who saw those who occupied and misused larger houses as both unfairly privileged and irresponsible. In fact, the immigrant ethnic community had been socially located, by the constraints of the housing market, in the worst possible social conditions and at the same time blamed for the whole social process.

This housing system changed to the second and later type of alternative system (Rex and Tomlinson, 1979) for two reasons. On the one hand, as dependents arrived to join male workers, the families themselves looked for better accommodation where they could bring up their children. On the other the City Council and central government developed the new policies outlined above to house them in the so-called improvement areas.

The houses involved in these areas had a certain class and status history. So long as the slums were standing they had been considered to be houses of a slightly better sort. Indeed, at the turn of the century, the areas in which they were situated had a certain grandeur about them, which was often marked by the building of a substantial park where the local residents could promenade and listen to the band on a Sunday afternoon. But the terraces around the park were now in decay and, with the completion of the major slum-clearance and redevelopment programme in the sixties, these areas included many of the worst remaining houses in the city. The newly-forming young White families responded to the situation by either getting on to the Council housing list and eventually getting housed in the public suburbia or getting mortgages on semi-detached suburban houses. They left behind only their ageing parents and those few who for one reason or another did not qualify for the suburban move. What remained was a population of whom a majority were often in the over sixty age group living alongside new neighbours who were willing to take over the abandoned houses.

The new neighbours were largely immigrants from overseas. Quite commonly in the London area, the West Midlands and part of the North these immigrants would constitute more than 20 per cent of the ward population, and in a few wards actually formed a majority of the population. It was these areas with 20 per cent and more of their population consisting of immigrant blacks which came to be thought of as primarily immigrant areas.

The first major group of settlers from the former colonial territories who arrived were from the West Indies. They were not a representatve cross section of the West Indian population, but men and women with minimum school qualifications who were unable to obtain entry to Canada and the United States. Hence, while West Indians in America as a whole fared better than Black Americans, the West Indian settlers in Britain were more like the native Black American migrants to the North from the Deep South. Moreover, since there were no affirmative action programmes equivalent to those which helped to stratify the Black American population in the sixties, what one had was a working class population employed in low grade factory jobs and in the public services doing what their children in due course came to call 'shitwork' (Pryce, 1979).

The immigrant generation amongst the West Indians were conservative in outlook (though they voted for the Labour Party) and many of them were keen churchgoers. About half of the church-goers affiliated to various Pentecostal and Holiness churches which combined ecstatic worship with a rigid Puritanism in daily life. But increasing numbers left the churches, and, amongst the rising adult generation, a new religion and culture arose, based upon the perception that West Indian people had been degraded by living for four hundred years in slavery or in a Babylonish captivity. The Jamaican religion of Rastafari came, for many young Blacks, to provide a source of inspiration to this group, equivalent to the Nation of Islam in the United States. It showed itself in the lyrics of reggae music and in the 'dreadlocks' and hats with Rasta colours often worn by the youth.

These cultural differences themselves appeared as threatening to the White population, since they were based upon a counter culture asserting itself aggressively against the culture of White colonialism. But conflict did not rest upon archaic cultural survivals only. The young Rastas were often boys who were unable to obtain employment either in the 'shit-jobs' occupied by their parents or in the mainstream, and, when they stood on street corners talking, or engaged in petty crime, they quickly found themselves in confrontation with the police. Although such young men were in a minority amongst their fellow countrymen, and there were many West Indians of the younger generation who became Anglicised and 'respectable', and some few, who despite all the obstacles, eventually achieved social mobility in the educational and occupational systems, it was these young Rastas who came for many Whites and, particularly for their elderly White neighbours, to symbolise the threat and the danger of West Indian settlement.

The second major group of settlers were from the Indian sub-continent. They included Punjabi-speaking Sikhs, clearly visible because of their turbans, Gujeratis, Pakistanis, Bangladeshis and Kashmiris, and were at least physically indistinguishable from Asians arriving for a new settlement from Kenya and Uganda. Except for the East Africans, most of the immigrant generation amongst these settlers spoke only limited English, so that despite the fact that there was a wide range of education amongst them, they were forced into the most unpleasant, heavy, industrial jobs, particularly in foundries and in textile industries. On the other hand, they also had considerable cultural resources and experience in succeeding within the niches of colonialism, and many of them began to achieve mobility through education, through taking over white-collar jobs and through shop-keeping and other wide-ranging business activities. Such mobility was achieved despite discrimination and, although these Asian communities were quick to mobilise against racist attack, they were, generally speaking, inclined to simply accept discrimination as part of the environment.

This story of Asian success, was, of course partial. Generally speaking, it was the East Africans and the Sikhs who made evident progress within the system, while at the other extreme Bangladeshis, poor Gujeratis and Pakistanis and the Mirpuris from Kashmnir faced relative educational failure and even conflict with the police. Nonetheless, overall the record of achievement was such that one might have expected that, other things being equal, the Asian communities would fairly quickly achieve assimilation. Other things, however, were not equal. Their English neighbours practised discrimination against all Asians, and amongst Asians they did not discriminate. Thus, when so-called 'Paki-bashing' became a virtual sport amongst delinquent working class White youth, it was directed against all Asians indiscriminately. Moreover, the very strength of Asian cultures kept their people apart. There was virtually no inter-marriage, and even sophisticated young University graduates found themselves under pressure to accept arranged marriages. Food habits also survived strongly and with these a great need developed for special groceries and other stores to sustain Asian culture. Thus, all in all, despite occupational and economic success, the Asians remained apart and were seen by many Whites as an alien wedge in the cities.

In the specific case of Birmingham, we thus had three communities co-existing very uneasily. The elderly Whites, without necessarily being racist in outlook, though some were, saw themselves and their homes and streets as having been abandoned by Central and Local Government to unacceptable and alien Black immigrants. The Asians with their strong traditions of family discipline were very critical of undisciplined West Indian youth. And Whites, particularly, but some West Indians, too, saw the alien ways of the Asians as menacing.

It might be asked at this point whether these observations on Birmingham are generalisable. Clearly, they can be in the case of colonial immigrants and they have some applicability to some of the immigrants in both Europe and America. It is particularly important to notice that in all such cases there may well be two distinct types of immigration: the immigration of those communities who are willing to accept low grade working class jobs; and the other kind of immigration in which there is a wide range of capacities for entering into niches within the total system. This distinction is important as such, whatever the ethnicity of a particular individual. But it is also important to notice that all immigrants who suffer from the stigma of colonialism are forced by racial discrimination into conditions of segregated inferiority and nowhere, more clearly, than in the housing system. Whether similar considerations apply to immigrants from non-colonial backgrounds, as in the case of Southern European Immigrants to North Europe, remains an open question. It is probably the case that they suffer from many of the hardships and difficulties mentioned for as long as a period of two generations, but that the acquisition of the language and the culture of their country of settlement enables them eventually to pass relatively unnoticed as part of the mainstream population. This process may however be arrested where the immigrants continue to be treated as 'guest workers' and the younger generation fail to acquire citizenship. Strangely, despite their manifest disadvantages, colonial immigrants in France and Britain have, at least in the initial stages of their settlement, enjoyed the advantages of citizenship.

To return to the British case, it must now be noted that the second stage of urban settlement which we have described gives way to a third. Despite the commitment of the society to urban improvement, and despite even the success of those policies, the conviction grows that deterioration is proceeding apace and that more radical measures are necessary. This is what happens when new policies for the inner city are elaborated.

There can be little doubt that one of the primary factors giving rise to the Inner City policy has been fear of ethnic and racial conflict. The urban riots which led to the burning of inner cities in the United States in the long hot summer of 1967 had a considerable impact on policy makers in all the advanced industrial societies. Policies for the poor and for the inner city had to be evolved so that what happened in the United States 'would not happen here.'

Nevertheless, the problem which was discussed was not that of racial and ethnic conflict. In democratic societies, there is, on the whole, an unwillingness to admit that concerns of this kind should determine public policy, and this is particularly true in Britain where a Fabian tradition of administration precludes the discussion of racial problems. What is discussed therefore is a problem of the environment. It is suggested that there are social processes peculiar to the inner city which require specific solutions, even though the areas to which they are thought to

71

apply are not strictly the inner city at all, but a secondary ring within which there is considerable immigrant settlement in bad housing conditions.

We have noted before that policies for urban change and development, in Britain at least, have been based for two generations on the idea of suburban dispersal. Industry was encouraged to move to the periphery and to New Towns and smaller industrial centres. This movement paralleled the residential move to suburbia. Generally, it was thought that the huge metropolitan centers were becoming inefficient and impossible to administer and that a new start in less congested conditions was desirable. Such policies, however, clearly implied either site and building abandonment in the inner areas or the concentration there of the unemployed and the less successful. The question which was posed, therefore, was whether the new atmosphere of confidence which had been generated in peri-urban settlement could now be injected into the inner city.

No one would deny that there is such a problem. But it runs parallel with the problem of ethnic and racial conflict, and, when Britain decided to sponsor major studies of the inner city, the areas chosen were Lambeth, an area of London marked by West Indian settlement, Small Heath, an area of Birmingham largely settled by Pakistanis and Mirpuris, and Liverpool 8, one of the oldest areas in which the Black British descendants of seamen were concentrated (Department of the Environment, 1977b). The problems of these areas were discussed as environmental problems and policies were suggested which would create inner city suburbs having the same character as the suburbs at the periphery. I have suggested that such policies involve in effect the reconquest of the so-called inner areas by the native population and especially by the native working class.

The White Paper, Policy for the Inner Cities, published in 1976 brings together the question of employment as related to the environment. It diagnoses the problem of the so-called inner city as essentially one of poverty, and argues for a reversal of the policy of industrial dispersal, so as to bring back jobs to the inner areas. It also proposed the continuation of the environment policies of the improvement and housing action areas at an increased pace and of the so-called Urban Programme, already established by the Home Office under which grants are given to local authorities and voluntary organisations for combatting poverty. It specifically excludes the question of racial discrimination from its brief, arguing that this is a separate matter for the separately-constituted Commission for Racial Equality. The whole of the new programme to be applied in particular designated areas is to be administered by Inner City Partnerships set up with participation from both Central and Local Government.

Argument about the Inner City policy has turned primarily on the question of the scale of funding with more radical politicians arguing that the funds devoted are mere 'peanuts' in relation to the scale of the problem involved. Less attention has been devoted to the question of who are to be its beneficiaries. Where this question has been discussed, the discussion has focussed on the distribution of grants under the Urban Programme, which constitutes only a small part of the total activity proposed for the partnerships. The question which is not discussed is how the existing population of the inner city is to benefit from employment and housing programmes.

On this last and crucial question the White Paper is ambiguous (Department of the Environemnt, para. 66-19, 1977b). It envisages that, when the Inner City becomes more prosperous so far as employment is concerned, there might well be a mismatch between the skills available and those required and suggests to the retired and the unskilled that they would do better to move to the periphery, which has an unduly low proportion of the unskilled.

That there is a problem of this kind for environmental and economic planning should by no means be denied. What, however, may be denied is the empirical basis for the assertion about the mismatch. Coupled with the failure to deal with the problem of racial and ethnic segregation and discrimination, the report might well be read as concluding that it is the immigrant populations who are mismatched with the new jobs becoming available, and that it is they who will be required to move. At its worst the White Paper could be read as advocating the dispersal of the unacceptable minority communities.

It is not necessary here to claim that such a policy will actually be carried through by the Planning Departments and Housing Departments concerned and it is, as a matter of fact, true that many of the grass roots officers are very much concerned with the welfare of immigrants. What is the case, however, is that the overall thrust of environmental planning is towards getting rid of what are perceived as the unacceptable elements of the inner city situation and that these are perceived as including the minority communities. Given this overall approach it is clear that the numerous detailed decisions involved allow for considerable discrimination against these communities if particular councils and their officers are so minded.

The general significance of what is being suggested here is that the substitution of planning and of a working class influence on planning decisions does not necesarily ensure that racial discrimination and oppression does not occur. In a free capitalist urban situation what happens is that the inner city areas are either left to rot or that they become the site of speculative development for the middle classes, the process called gentrification. In the semiplanned situation which exists in Britain, however, what happens might be described as a process of public gentrification. Having produced a zone of relatively segregated immigrant settlement with all the problems that that involves, the thrust of the new policy is towards the dispersal of these communities and the reconquest of those areas so that they come to conform with working class standards.

There are, of course, inherent contradictions in this policy. The idea of establishing suburban standards in the inner city is modified by a realistic recognition that this must be an inferior type of area and there is no clear indication as to where the dispersed populations are to go, except 'away'. But, in any case, the policy of bringing such areas up to Welfare State standards is not particularly popular with right wing politicians, who do not care overmuch about these standards anyway. Not surprisingly, therefore, the Conservative Government of 1979 began to withdraw support from the Inner City policy and to substitute for it the notion of Urban Free Enterprise Zones, in which expensive subsidies and inducements to industry and housing would disappear and free enterprise would be encouraged by the withdrawal of frustrating bureaucratic controls.

If the new Conservative policy were sustained for a fairly long period, what one would see would not be the reconquest of the inner city for working class and Welfare State standards, but rather the spread of a policy of unrestrained free enterprise, a policy which actually exists in the inner city, to other areas. The extreme version of Conservative policy in this direction, as in others, is not to fight against discrimination by ensuring that there is equal access to Welfare State services, but rather to achieve equality by eliminating these services. This is particularly evident in the policy of withdrawing subsidies to Council housing and selling off as much as possible of the existing stock of Council housing to sitting tenants. Obviously this rests upon an ideological conviction that, in the long run, free enterprise rather than planning and subsidy offers the best hope of raising standards. Obviously, also, the opposite view may be maintained, namely that without considerable interference in the free market for land, housing and employment, the weakest will go to the wall.

It would appear that, in practice, the new policies will contain contradictions just as did the more socialist Inner City policies. Free enterprise, like interventionist planning, is likely to be modified by racial discrimination. This could have led to the application of free enterprise policies to the inner city areas which were the focus of Labour concern, if, in fact, the Conservatives were really cynical about their own policies and actually wished to offer an inferior deal to the ethnic minorities. Since, however, they do believe in them, they offer their benefits not to the minorities but to working class populations by establishing the free enterprise zones in areas not marked by overwhelming immigrant settlement.

The final outcome, if there is one, of these alternating and conflicting policies is as yet by no means clear. The lesson which they offer, however, is that racial discrimination and oppression are not uniquely the consequence either of free enterprise or of planning. The need to study racial and class discrimination as part of the total urban system remains, whichever ideology prevails, and whatever policy is pursued. A change in this situation would be dependent on presently underprivileged minorities exercising political power on their own behalf.

One final question which remains to be discussed is whether the approach to these problems which has been adopted here is not too voluntaristic and moralistic. We have assumed here that it is worthwhile concentrating attention on the actual decision makers or gatekeepers of the urban system, as though they were the ultimate decision makers, and that their decisions could have been otherwise. The new Marxist school of urban sociology urges a more systemic approach and classifies those who adopt these approaches as 'the managerial school' (Lambert, Blackaby and Parris, 1978).

According to the neo-marxists the problem which we have to face is that of the function of the policies we have been discussing for the capitalist system in its more sophisticated forms (Castells, 1977). In these more sophisticated forms, capitalism requires considerable intervention by the national and the local state (Cockburn, 1977) and considerable public spending or collective consumption to ensure that the labour supply is reproduced.

There is considerable value in this broad general approach. Gatekeepers do not have total leeway in the decisions which they make. They are constrained by such factors as the cost of land and the rate of interest on loans. Moreover there has been, at the highest policy making levels, a concern with the condition of labour which stems, not from humanitarian considerations, but rather from the need to mobilise and control a labour force. Nonetheless, two kinds of criticism of the neo-marxist approach are in order.

The first criticism is that, if the Marxist theses are to be sustained, they require empirical evidence, and that this evidence can only be obtained through the study of actual decisions made both at local and national levels. Such decisions, moreover, must, especially in a Marxist approach, be based upon a realistic recognition of the effect which class struggle and working class power has on the national and local state. A failure to look at these empirical details could only leave us with a dogmatic and monolithic theoretical model of the workings of capitalism in the urban context.

The second criticism is that the neo-marxists in their concentration on the 'social reproduction of labour' have failed to indicate in detail what kind of labour force it is which is being reproduced. A capitalist society may indeed develop social policies affecting the whole of the working class, but, if it is in the nature of that system at a particular stage in the process of accumulation to require a divided working class, it is surely to be expected that differential policies will be developed to deal with different types of workers. The problem here is that the neo-marxists have remained at a high level of general theorising without getting down to difficult and embarrassing specifics.

All in all, the study of the urban system since the days of the early Chicago school has had to undergo considerable modification to take account of other countries' experience, and of the influence of intervention by central and local government. What this chapter seeks to do is to use a particular empirical example drawn from post-war Britain to pose new questions and to give to the theories originally proposed by the Chicago school a wider empirical validity.

VII The theory of the sociology of education and race relations research in schools

The researcher who approaches the problem of the effect of the educational system on race relations is faced, as in most fields of research, with an infinite inflow of factual information. There is, therefore, a problem of selection of what is relevant and, therefore, a need for theory. On the other hand, to predefine too precisely what the relevant questions are in terms of some highly abstract theoretical schema would undoubtedly lead to the oversight of important data. Closely related to this particular dilemma, moreover, is that of choosing between the theoretical constructs of the sociologist and those of the participant actor. On the one hand, the theory of the sociology of education defined in terms of abstract systems theory or in terms of data categories fails to reflect the actual processes of the construction of social reality by participant actors. On the other, the phenomenological or ethnomethodological approach, while capturing that which is evanescent, fails to do justice to the concept of social structure.

The resolution of these problems must lie in the emergence of sociological theory in the course of ongoing research. One starts with a range of value-oriented interests. In this case they may be broadly defined as those which affect the relationships of domination and subordination between ethnic groups. Formulating these problems inevitably involves the formulation of theoretical categories which capture the uniqueness of the situation. On the other hand, there is no reason why a theoretically literate sociologist should not be able to relate these categories to the categories of the theoretical sociology of education. In the process of relating these two, the validity of both will be put to test. In a parallel field, I found it necessary in studying housing to develop the concept of housing class. That concept can be readily seen to have its place within a wider analysis of life chances and group formation connected with the attempt to improve life chances.

The sort of theory which we should pursue should avoid the extremes of both systems theory and ethnomethodology. This by no means implies that it should not concern itself with the relation between one institutional area and another. To some extent sociology will always be functionalist in so far as it does this. It should, however, always be prepared to recognise that the outside pressures on a sub-system might arise from group interests rather than the needs of the system, and that within the sub-system the particular structures are only partially determined and are affected by the countervailing pressures arising from different participant actors. Per contra, it must be pointed out in the face of those who lay emphasis solely on the manufacture of social categories to the extent of denying that there is any structure apart from that which is willed into existence at a particular moment, that the choices available to individuals in defining their situation are subject to real external social constraints. While it may be important to note the way in which selection processes operate, it is also important to discover facts such as the relative success in the selection process of individuals of differing class and ethnic backgrounds.

Given these presuppositions about the bearing of theory on research in the field of education and race relations, two sets of questions suggest themselves. The first deals with the question 'what social processes are being carried on within schools and other educational institutions?' The second, not wholly separable from the first, concerns the way in which decision-makers, strategically placed within the system and outside of it, affect the basic social processes called 'educational'.

The first field of enquiry in the sociology of education in Britain was in accordance with the empiricist London tradition, that which studied the relationship between education and social class. The dissatisfaction which arose in relation to these studies was with their obsessive preoccupation with correlations between educational achievement and very narrowly defined social characteristics. This dissatisfaction, however, can be over stated. Much was accomplished in the Floud-Halsey tradition (Floud Halsey and Martin 1956) to reveal the relation between educational processes and social class and status. Moreover, in a study concerned with racial and ethnic discrimination, where the life chances of major ethnic communal groupings are at stake, there can be no doubt that one objective of sociological research should be to study the educational process as a selective process, assigning to individuals of different ethnic origins differing life chances. There is no reason at all why hard data on the differential rate of achievement in matters such as reading age, success in selective examinations, and other data recorded in schools should not be sought out as a central part of the study. It should be possible to use the resources of the city statistical office in this matter as well as those of the education department, particular schools within the area of study, and other agencies such as the youth employment service. The collection of such data is not simply a formal exercise to provide a 'sound statistical base', but is theoretically important because these statistical categories do affect real sociological processes which only a totally abstracted phenomenological intellectual would wish to deny.

With this much said, however, no one would wish to deny that the manufacture of social reality and statistical categories in the actual day to day processes of selection is an additional important topic for study. For example, the bare statistic that West Indians on the average have a lower reading age than British born children, may, taken by itself, be too readily interpreted as implying some kind of genetic inadequacy on the part of West Indians. An analysis of the actual circumstances in which scores are assigned for reading age would very quickly reveal the significance of these statistics. In the theoretically extreme case one might find that a process is operated in which the tests of reading age are so designed as to ensure that West Indians will be placed in lower categories. The objective of studying the construction of social reality, however, is not simply to discover the malign intent on the part of the classifiers, it is simply part of systematic social research. It should, therefore, be a routine part of social investigation to analyse the way in which each statistical category has, in fact, been constructed, and perhaps also to note other selective processes which operate in practice without ever finding their place within the official statistics.

A much more sophisticated understanding of the nature of the selective process has occurred within the British sociology of education, particularly as a result of the work of Bernstein (Bernstein 1970, 1971, 1973 and 1975). He and his colleagues have raised, firstly, the question of the effects of communicative processes in education, and, secondly, the way in which knowledge is socially distributed. Little need be said here about the importance of linguistic studies. There is, of course, a danger that such studies may be used ideologically to provide somewhat thin proofs that the natural language of inferior groups debars them from educational progress. This is true in the study of working class and middle class language in which the educational value of middle class language has been grossly overestimated in some discussions of the importance of Bernstein's work, with the result that emphasis has been placed upon the importance of destroying and replacing working class language in order to ensure working class educational success. This might very well be simply part of a total process of ideological class domination. In so far as this is true, it is even more likely to be the case where the language of ethnic minorities is criticised and used as an explanation for the inadequacy of educational achievement of these minorities. On the other hand, if these reservations are taken into account, there can be no doubt whatever that the study of the way in which creole English functions in everyday life and in the school situation, and still more the way in which having to use a second language for educational purposes affects educational achievement, is a prime topic of study. Much information can be gathered here by considering the way in which special language teaching programmes operate. Again, it is necessary to approach such studies with appropriate ethnomethodological caution, noting the ways in which those charged with linguistic education programmes bring to their work social and political assumptions about what it is that they have to do.

On the question of the social distribution of knowledge, the prime point here is perhaps a Durkheimian one. This is that, since it is no longer possible for every individual in a society to possess all of its knowledge, the functioning of the society requires that each individual should, as it were, have fitted into his head part of that total knowledge which leads to his functioning as a particular kind of role player within a larger social system. In saying this, one need not, however, accept the Durkheimian assumption that what is achieved through the social distribution of knowledge is organic solidarity. It is perfectly possible to look at the process of the social distribution of knowledge as part of a total process of social stratification. That is to say, the kind of knowledge with which a particular individual is equipped may lead to his being incapable of participation in the social system except in inferior roles.

The analysis of the social distribution of knowledge divides into both the study of form and the study of content. So far as the study of form is concerned, it is very important to notice that knowledge is organised in different types of unit with more or less segregation of one unit from another in different educational situations. When school reorganisation and curriculum reform takes place, the formal structure of transmitted knowledge changes. It matters enormously, therefore, if it is found that a local authority proposes that most of its children in school should have less subject-structured contexts. The effect of possessing one of these kinds of knowledge structure rather than another is as important as the use of one type of language rather than another by children entering school.

A much more direct and important aspect of the social distribution of knowledge, however, is the very simple question of what knowledge is given and what knowledge is concealed from students in different kinds of educational institutions. To put this in terms of a very simple example, it was not normally part of the education of a working class child in pre-war schools to be told how to buy stocks and shares, to buy and sell a house, or even to drive a motor car. These bits of knowledge and these skills were part of the normal equipment of those who possessed stocks and shares, houses, and property. Entry into the class of those who possessed this kind of property could be restricted by the denial of the appropriate forms of knowledge. In the case of inferior ethnic minorities in schools, they might also be denied forms of knowledge which would enable them to compete effectively with the majority, or to organise to resist the majority. Of considerable importance in this regard is the process of education in the Caribbean itself. So far as information is available on this point, it would seem to be the case that West Indian students were given a totally distorted and ideological picture of the nature of English society and of attitudes held within it towards black people.

A more general area of investigation under the general heading of 'what the educational process is achieving for the larger social system' is the study of the reasons for failure by members of minority groups to achieve the highest qualifications. It is important here to look both at cases in which no particular effort is made to positively discriminate in favour of minorities and those cases in which special programmes are instituted for the minorities. Where no special effort is made it should be possible to detect the ways in which structural factors and prejudice on the psychological and sociology of knowledge levels lead to lower achievement by minorities. But the more perplexing and difficult problem is that of failure in those circumstances in which, despite the employment of the best available techniques in terms of educational expertise, achievement remains low. In these cases what has to be done is to analyse the causes of minority resistance to participation in a basically competitive process. This may involve a study of the relationship between schooling systems in the immigrant's homeland and schooling systems in the country of immigration, with a view to discovering the degree to which non-achievement is the product of frustrated expectation. It may also involve an analysis of the personal and social disorganisation involved in positing an educational process based upon the destruction or setting aside of indigenous culture patterns.

An area of considerable importance for this investigation is that of the effect upon educational performance of continued rootedness in a minority culture. Thus, we need to know the extent to which firm commitment to Indian and Pakistani language, religion, and culture at home, coupled with an instrumental attitude towards education in England, facilitates educational attainment compared with the attainment of native born children and West Indian children. In the case of West Indian children, it is important to discover the degree to which they can be said to have a language, culture, ideology, or religion different from the English, or whether there is a defensive counter-culture based upon the concept of black power which might have an effect upon educational attainment.

So far as this last matter is concerned, it is interesting to note that a continuing problem in schools is that of the religious education syllabus. It is no longer the case that this is solely concerned with the transmission of agreed 'decent Christian values'. It is widely recognised that in a multi-ethnic society, part of religious education must involve the acquisition of the knowledge of the culture and traditions of minorities. On the other hand, it is worth noting that, while it has been seriously posited in Birmingham that the study of Communism as a form of religion should be a part of the religious education syllabus, responses to the teaching of Black Studies, where it has occurred, have on the whole been panicky and negative. The important question here is to look at what Talcott Parsons would call the operation of 'the ultimate value system' of the society in the schools through the religious education syllabus and other related types of teaching, e.g. in history.

We may sum up the major areas of study which are concerned with what is happening in the schools, therefore, under the following heads:

1. The process of selection as indicated by statistics of attainment in various test situations.
2. The social construction of reality which lies behind the statistical categories.
3. The effect of language use by different groups on their capacity to perform successfully in the educational system.
4. The social distribution of knowledge looked at in terms of the forms within which it is organised, including here the study of the formal structure of the curriculum both in particular schools and in consortia of schools, with a view to detecting educational advantages and disadvantages which the system promotes.
5. The social distribution of knowledge looked at in terms of content and the amount of knowledge of the real world of power and how to attain and use that power which is made available to various groups.
6. The problem of alternative explanations of minority group failure, including the study of differential expectations of the school system and the effect upon educational attainment of rootedness in a minority culture.
7. The study of the ultimate value system in education, particularly as it is reflected in the changing pattern of the religious education syllabus.

It should be noted that what we have been discussing above by no means involves an abandonment of the study of educational systems or of the wider social system in favour of undirected, subjective studies. What we should be studying in schools is the pattern of the educational process as a whole. It should be clear, moreover, that this educational and social process appears to be considerably different from that idealised process which is posited in the policy documents of the decision-makers. Nonetheless, an additional factor in the situation on the ground is precisely the existence of this idealised definition, and it is also true that decision-making on educational policy reflects the constraints which are placed upon the educational system by politically organised society. It should be recognised, therefore, that any study of education and race relations would be incomplete if the topics already mentioned were not pursued through looking at the way in which they are discussed in educational policy-making, and it is also true that the ongoing educational and social processes which we have discussed will be affected from time to time by policy decisions made for reasons external to these particular processes.

It is possible to look at the operation of an educational system in a particular city in terms of general research on the sociology of educational systems, in terms of national educational policy, and in terms of local educational policy. Further, one might extend this process by looking at the activities of headmasters and even individual teachers as educational decision-makers. The best starting point, however, in order to establish the differentiation between the educational process and those forces which affect it is probably the discussion of educational policy at local authority level. Here one can see both the way in which local decison-makers respond to particular contingencies and the way in which they reinterpret national policy directives. The best procedure, therefore, with regard to the study of educational policy making would be to make an initial study of operative policies so that one would both obtain some useful hints as to what the ongoing problems within the social processes of education were, and at the same time see what the external pressures on the educational and social processes were. It would however, become necessary to return to the analysis of educational policy with a more sophisticated range of questions after greater understanding of the actual educational and social process in the schools had been obtained from a sociological point of view.

VIII Equality of opportunity and the ethnic minority child

One can begin to understand the role of the schools in determining the destiny of minority children by looking in turn at how the educational system in a country like Great Britain deals with a number of basic issues. These include the allocation of school places particularly in secondary schools, the medium of instruction at the moment of entry to schools, the teaching of mother tongue, the teaching of English as a second language at basic levels, the maintenance of minority cultures, the teachng of English as a second language at more sophisticated levels, the provision of courses at examination levels in minority languages, history and culture, specific teaching to combat racism and the modification of the curriculum as a whole and for all children in ways that give recognition to minority cultures.

The allocation of school places or the allocation of children to specific schools has interestingly dropped off the agenda so far as minority children are concerned. There was, of course, and still is a debate which goes on about the assignment of native born working class children to schools. Middle class parents have usually taken care to locate their homes within the catchment areas of schools where there are less rough working class children and the system as a whole has always involved some degree of segregation. What has happened in recent years, however, is the emergence of further differentiation within what are largely working class schools between problem inner city schools and those in longer established and often suburban working class schools. The children of immigrant minorities have been heavily concentrated in the worst of the inner-city schools.

It might be thought that the proposal for bussing which emerged in Ealing when the first classes with 30 per cent plus Asian students emerged was precisely the sort of policy which could be said to be promoting equality of educational opportunity. The policy certainly seemed to have a respectable pedigree in the American Civil Rights movement. Study of the actual cases in which bussing was proposed in England, however, serves to throw doubt on this. What was being discussed was not that Asian and West Indian children in these schools were not enjoying equality of opportunity, but that there were increasing numbers of schools in which English working class children were being held back by the problem of having non-English speaking classmates and suffering the stigma of being educated in Black schools. The basic answer to the question as where the surplus of Black children should go was really simply 'Away'. When 'away' was seen to mean that they would crop up in other schools as well, and when they would have had to be replaced by other children bussed in to inferior schools, the pressure for bussing quickly died away.

In fact, as matters are at present, minority children are likely to suffer one of two undesirable fates. Either they form a small minority in White schools or they find themselves heavily segregated in Black schools. So far as the former is concerned the schools have rarely been able to respond to the variety of problems faced by the minority children. Faced with growing resource constraints they have barely been able to cope with what might be called normal problems. Below certain levels in their minority numbers they may not be eligible for the so-called Section 11 money which Government provides for the education of minority children and will be forced to assign minority children and their problems to whatever problem solving organisations they have. There may be more or less sophistication in the way in which different Head teachers approach this problem but the temptation must surely be to see the problems of minority children as remedial problems. Classification and labelling of this kind will appeal particularly if the teachers involved are predisposed to make racist judgements. There are very slight signs indeed of the problem being addressed in terms of some professional ethic.

If what has just been said is true some might then be inclined to argue that the problems of West Indian and Asian children - or more strictly the children of West Indian and Asian immigrants - will be best dealt with in functionally specialised and segregated schools. Unfortunately one cannot accept this quietly complacent view. We now have schools in inner city areas of London and the Midlands where the percentage of these children is between 90 and 100 per cent. American experience reminds us that in the 58 years between the Plessey vs Ferguson and the Brown vs the Board of Education judgements, the American courts concluded that education which was separate was inherently unequal. That conclusion was reached in the light of a huge weight of evidence. We have no such evidence here partly because our school system depends so much on Head teacher autonomy and partly because social scientists have not yet made up for the deficiency of centralised records by systematically researching the schools. What is allowed to count as evidence is usually the teachers' own estimate of their performance. In arguing about this 'evidence' we would no doubt concede that there are some devoted and skilled teachers who want above all to ensure that all their children have a fair chance. But, prima facie, since the teaching is hard and unrewarding, even where there is some inducement provided by way of special increments, many of the teachers who gravitate towards these schools are simply those who can't get better positions. And there are surely also likely to be some racists and paternalists who see the role of the slum teacher and the teacher of Blacks as one quite removed from that of teaching for academic success in a 'normal' school. Quite often teachers in these schools see themselves as running 'remedial' schools or as providing special teaching directed towards passing so-called C.S.E. Mode Three examinations.

Apart from anything else the segregation of Asian and West Indian children together in the same schools means that two quite different sets of minority educational problems are being dealt with simultaneously. Asian children, whether successful or not, face problems of a linguistic and cultural kind and come from families with a strong positive attitude towards the instrumental aspects of British education. The West Indian children come from a culture which is a regional variant of English culture marked and marred by the heritage of slavery. Moreover within each of these groups and within the sub-groups amongst them there are numerous variations. It is surely absurd to suppose that there is something called Black education which can deal with all of these diverse problems. Quite probably there are teachers within the system who know how diverse the problems are, but they must be aware more than anyone how unsophisticated the response of their schools has been in understanding the diversity.

Obviously problems of disadvantage and inequality arise for minority children because of the kinds of institution in which they find themselves. But, with that understood, there is an additional problem of language. Even if there were not such questions of disadvantage therefore, some minority children, and especially Asian children would face problems at the moment of entry. These problems are of three kinds. There is the problem for the non-English speaking child of approaching his school work with the linguistic capacity he or she does command. There is the problem of maintaining his or her skill in the mother tongue, and there is the problem of acquiring sufficient English to be able to work with English as the medium of instruction. These three problems require separate consideration.

Three approaches have been adopted to the question of the language of instruction at the moment of entry into the school. Children have been sent to special centres for English instruction. Peripatetic teachers have serviced schools with non-English speaking children. And, finally and worst of all, the children have simply been left to cope with English as best they can. All of these techniques work to some extent, but surely they are all unsophisticated, callous and cruel. They fail to cope with the basic problem facing all school children which is that at the outset they have not merely to learn but to learn to learn. A child who has to cope within the first years of his or her schooling both with acquiring a new language and starting the learning process lives in something of a nightmare world. No doubt the nightmare becomes less and less frightening as time goes on. But at the best the outcome will be that the child no longer presents such a severe problem to the school. His or her capacity for future learning may however have been permanently damaged. Certainly this situation mocks the very notion of equality of opportunity.

There is, of course, an alternative. It has been quite widely adopted in countries such as Sweden, has existed for some time in England as far as non-English speaking European children are concerned, and is just beginning in one or two areas for Asian children. This is that at the outset the non-English speaking child receives his education in the medium of the mother tongue. The learning process then starts and within that it is possible to introduce English as a second language by stages. In that way language acquisition takes place within the learning process and not in opposition to it. It should be noted that the aim of education in the mother tongue here is not to try to create linguistic apartheid, but its very opposite, namely to help the child eventually to learn much more effectively in English.

Still under this same head of the use of mother tongue we have to note what has been the major linguistic problem in England, namely that of the late entrant to the system. Here, however, the same principles would apply. To first be withdrawn from a class to learn English and then be placed back in it and left to catch up with the work virtually guarantees that although the minority child learns to speak English he or she will be placed near the bottom of a class. What would be necessary to ensure equality of opportunity would be a continuation of instruction in the mother tongue with the gradual introduction of English to the point at which the child could be placed in a normal class on something like equal terms.

To suggest the establishment of institutions which could cope with educational problems as well as language teaching on this scale would immediately produce the reply that resources were not available on this scale. Yet the problem posed by the assimilation of tens of thousands of non-English speaking children are such that, had equality of opportunity been taken seriously as a goal, institutions of this kind were credible. The actual type of provision clearly fitted the need to train an underclass without disturbing the day to day routine of lower class schools too much. Since, together with with discussion of bussing and then the de facto acceptance of segregation, the provision of language teaching in withdrawal classes was the main form of policy response to immigration, it seems to be the case that the creation of such an underclass was all that was envisaged.

A quite different question from instruction in the mother tongue was that of mother tongue maintenance. This has a quite literal meaning in that it deals with the problem of enabling Asian children to continue to talk to their mothers. As matters stand many Asian children, having to use English to deal with the major matters of education and life, lose the facility to speak the language of their parents, with considerable disruption of their home life and the imposition of severe strain on the cultural and personality level. There has been some debate about the question of whether the maintenance of bilingualism retards learning. Common sense suggests to many administrators that it does. Research in the area, however, points in the opposite direction. As in the case of instruction in the mother tongue, so in this case, it is interesting that the need has been far more readily recognised in the case of Italian and other European children. Different standards seem to have been applied in assessing the needs of Asians.

The third problem mentioned above has already been implicitly dealt with. Emphasis upon mother tongue teaching as a problem by no means implies that there is not a serious problem of providing for instruction in English as a second language. The aim of achieving equality of opportunity implies the development of sophisticated teaching methods and of ensuring that this does not mean a retardation in the general educational process. Possibly it could be argued that those who have to surmount the hurdle of learning a new language should go back a year at school. What is not compatible with equal opportunity is a policy which places the non-English speaking child at the bottom of the class. Generally speaking provision in this area is such that those authorities which have simply provided withdrawal centres are thought to be in the vanguard. All that these centres can do by themselves, however, is to solve the administrative problems of schools. They do not solve the problems of minority children in a competitive educational system.

The problems of Asian children in the language area are reproduced in a weaker but still significant form for West Indian Creole speaking families. One might not argue here for instruction in Creole, except perhaps in infant classes, but the stresses and strains of West Indian life are such that effective operation at school and in the home and community requires the development of a healthy bilingualism.

There is obviously a cultural problem parallel to the linguistic problem which we have been discussing. A case can and should be made for culture maintenance along with language maintenance. There are, however, real difficulties here because of the place usually occupied by social and cultural studies in the curriculum, particularly at the lower secondary levels. If it is already the case in a school that such studies are provided simply to solve the problem of the less bright children, then fitting Asian and Caribbean studies into the curriculum in that particular slot could simply be a way of reinforcing any tendency to inequality. If moreover the subject was taught in a paternalistic way by White teachers it could have little positive value.

A particular set of problems relates to the teaching of Black Studies to West Indian children in schools. It is here that the problems of paternalism are at their most acute. The movement which goes under the name of Black Consciousness in all its many forms is a movement of the most profound importance in the West Indian islands and in migrant West Indian communities. It is a movement which seeks to rectify the cultural damage done to those forcibly transported from Africa to the plantations and, inevitably, it involves an element of political resistance. It is extremely unlikely that White teachers in a White school setting would understand and be able to interpret this culture in its full significance. What tends to be offered therefore under the heading of Black studies is a castrated form of this culture which lays emphasis upon its safe and stereotypical products such as steel bands. Not surprisingly serious students of the educational problems of West Indian children have seen education of this type in schools as a distraction which at worst labels West Indian children as different and inferior and at best is a distraction from the more serious aspects of education.

The conclusion to which one is led is that the maintenance of minority culture is best left to those who believe in it, that is to say to the adult members of the community involved through supplementary education, unless in rare cases there are schools in which the subject is understood and the place given to it in the curriculum is such that it does not imply inferiority. Supplementary schools on the other hand do in fact have a very important role to play in the educational system and deserve financial support from any government committed to equality of opportunity. Not merely do they guarantee a healthy bi-culturalism which is beneficial to the society as a whole as well as to the educational progress of the children involved. They also provide a valuable setting in which successful remedial education can occur. Not surprisingly many West Indian supplementary schools have found a function for themselves, not so much in teaching Black Studies courses, but much more in teaching basic skills in an atmosphere free of the cultural biases and sometimes implicit racism which inhibits children's progess in schools.

Nothing which has been said above on these issues, however, should be taken to suggest that all children of West Indian and Asian parents should be forced into following a bi-cultural educational programme. Increasingly these children in schools insist that they are British and want to be treated as such. While some of them and their parents may see such bi-culturalism as an essential value to be maintained, the matter should be one of choice. Skin-colour should not determine educational rights. What should do are the changing values of the children involved. What they most want if they are given equal opportunity and have attained the necessary skills is to gain full recognition amongst their peers and by their teachers.

What we have been discussing so far is the provision of the kind of setting in which young children in primary schools or in the early stages of secondary education are protected from unnecessary psychological strains so that they can cope adequately with the learning process. This, however, is only a starting point. In the crucial selective stages of secondary education, and perhaps particularly in new comprehensive schools, it is essential that children should not merely have English but that their English should become more sophisticated so that they can use the language in a discriminating way in order to cope with high level Arts and Science courses. To learn to speak a language in a basic way and to gain acceptance in the majority culture and society of schoolchildren is by no means to be able to compete at the higher academic levels. The sociology of education in Britain has dealt extensively with the difficulties faced by English working class children in acquiring the kind of language necessary to succeed at the higher levels. The child from an ethnic minority, however, finds that he has to make a double transition, first from his own language and culture to that of the Engish school and peer group culture and then from that position to one in which he has the linguistic capacity to cope with work in the higher levels. The answer to this set of difficulties lies clearly in the development of an adequate English as a Second Language, Stage Two, programme. Yet, as Little and Willey found in their survey (Little and Willey, 1981), this aspect of provision for minority children has, as yet, hardly been developed. Asian children do in fact cope with these difficulties and, if the Rampton evidence (Department of Education and Science, 1981) is to be taken seriously, cope well enough to do as well or slightly better than their English peers. This degree of competitive success, however, by no means shows that there is not a great deal of ability being wasted because of linguistic deficiency.

The final set of problems which a programme of multi-cultural education has to face deals not simply with the elimination of technical and psychological barriers to competitive success in an ongoing system. Rather it deals with the schools evaluation of minority peoples and their culture. Taking for granted that the schools must evaluate the success of children in coping with the demands of British society and without any wish to create a kind of cultural apartheid, however, we must now ask whether the educational system can ensure that minority cultures have their place within the total system. Clearly we do not have and will not have the kind of cultural situation which exists in, say, Brussels or Quebec, in which two or more cultures have actual political equality. But to say this is by no means to say that our society cannot be multi-cultural in the sense of giving academic validation to minority cultures.

In a perceptive piece written for the Association of Teachers of Social Science, Jennifer Williams (1979) has pointed out that minority cultures have been given a place in the low-status uncertificated parts of the curriculum only. The obvious answer to this is that they should be given their place at high status and certificated levels.

What is not wanted clearly is that Asian and West Indian children should be offered soft options so that they can get O and A Levels of some kind. Such qualifications would be of little value in the world of work anyway. To say this, however, is by no means to say that there is not a place for academically rigorous courses in Asian and Caribbean languages and culture which merit equal respect with courses in European languages and culture. If courses are provided at this level the effect on such education as exists in minority languages and culture lower down the school would be immediate. They would no longer simply imply a way in which the less bright child might fill in his time but would have their place in a sustained programme of academic training. It would also be possible at this level to take on board some of the political difficulties which beset courses in minority culture at the lower levels. The test of acceptability would not be a political one of whether or not cultural values are subversive. It might be argued that it is in the nature of cultural values to be subversive. What, however, would be the case is that the clash of political standpoints would be rigorously subjected to scrutiny within an academic discipline. For all the anti-working class bias of History courses in Britain in the past, it has been possible to develop History syllabuses in which central themes of working class struggle have found their place in a rigorous academic curriculum. Similarly courses in Asian and Afro-

Caribbean Studies would give serious and critical attention to the themes of Colonialism, Slavery and Racism.

Pure Language courses would also have their place in this curriculum. Just as those who study French history are advised to learn French Language at the higher levels, so Asian children will naturally want to learn their own languages along with courses in their history and culture. Some may even wish to learn related scholarly languages, just as English children learn Classics and it is not surprising that some Muslim educationalists call for provision and recognition of courses in Arabic. Of course not every Asian child would wish to take these courses any more than every English child who survives to O and A Level wishes to take Modern Languages or Classics. But it would be an option and the existence of such an option would do much to institutionalise respect for the minority culture.

On the whole it is not the examining boards which stand in the way of these developments. They already provide examinations in Asian languages and would be open to proposals to develop examining in the area of Asian and Afro-Caribbean culture and history. Basically the problem is one of resources and teacher initiative. While there are, clearly, resource constraints in providing for minority subjects of all kinds, it should not be impossible to ensure within a local authority area that courses of the kind envisaged are provided on a centralised basis.

It has been suggested here that the provision of higher level courses in Minority Languages and Culture will have a beneficial effect upon courses lower down the school. Equally they might have a powerful effect on the two other types of provision which we have to discuss, namely, teaching against racism and the 'deracialisation' of the curriculum as a whole. Nothing could accelerate the development of the curriculum in these directions more than the accreditation of minority cultures within the credentialling system.

Teaching against racism can have a similar beneficial effect within the system as a whole. Every British school has a problem of racism. The Rampton Committee dwelt upon teacher racism and perhaps overrated the importance of its more overt forms. But the fact is that what we have to cope with is a situation in which, although racism is formally and legally regarded as undesirable and illegitimate, we live within a culture in which racism is implicit in the thinking of many British parents and children as well as teachers.

A poor answer to the problem is to provide what might be called 'Sunday-school lessons' in anti-racism. Such research as there is suggested that lessons of this kind are, if anything, likely to be counter-productive (Stenhouse 1979). We do, however, recognise that some kind of political education has its part to play in the curriculum at all levels including the highest and, given the formal commitment of our society to anti-racism, it is surely not far-fetched to suggest that within Government and Politics courses, this theme should have a reasonably central place. It accords after all both with the Socialist theme of the brotherhood of man and with the Tory theme of One Nation. Here, as in the case of the teaching of minority cultures what is required is the institutionalisation of a theme through its inclusion at the most serious and recognised point in the curriculum. It is a theme which belongs in the core of the curriculum and one which should be found at the highest levels.

Finally, it has to be noted that the response of many educationalists to suggestions about structural reform of the curriculum to accommodate minority children is to say that what is wanted is not special and separate provision but reform of the curriculum as a whole and for all children to take account of the fact that we are living in a multi-cultural society. This can be very misleading. Unless the thrusts of multi-culturalism and equality of opportunity for minority children are deliberately institutionalised it is unlikely that anything will happen to the syllabus as a whole and the protestations of those who talk in general terms about a suitable syllabus for a multi-cultural society are all too often a cover for an intention to do nothing.

If, however, all the other elements of a programme to ensure equality of opportunity and respect for the minority child have found their place within the system the more general problem of curriculum reform remains. Text-books, syllabuses and exam-schemes have to be revised. What one would like to hear, however, are concrete and specific proposals for doing this rather than general affirmations. Much better that we should hear of concrete proposals for revision of the history and literature syllabuses to give due weight to the problems of the Indian sub-continent and the Caribbean than that we should be invited to agree that even the Maths syllabus should be revised in the direction of Mathematics for all Mankind.

What is required here is that this problem should be dealt with seriously. What we have at present is simply a concern for developing multi-cultural books and materials usually for use at the lower levels. Is it not possible that some of the many resource centres which are growing up to meet this demand could enlarge their scope and become the centres in which precise proposals for syllabus reform could be developed?

What we have set out here is the sort of agenda which would have to be tackled if the question of equality of opportunity for the minority child, including the theme of equality of respect for minority peoples and their culture, was taken seriously. It should be absolutely clear that in terms of these goals actual provision falls woefully short. What we see on the whole is a system which has responded by addressing those problem areas in which minority children pose problems for an ongoing system rather than one which addresses the new and specific problems of the minority child. Still worse, the effect is to provide a system in which many minority children actually fail by the criteria which matter and, through failing, are forced into the situation, if not of an underclass, at least of an excluded class. In fact it could be argued that if this were the acknowledged aim of the system it could be regarded as highly effective and it is this point which is often made of Sociologists of Education and Marxists in what appear to practitioners to be cynical comments on their work.

It is certainly not the aim of this paper to deny the genuine idealism of many practitioners. What we have sought to do here is simply to apply systematic critical standards to their achievements rather than their ideals and to show how the constraints of the system drive even their most idealistic aims in unintended directions. This is even more true when we turn to a consideration of the effective as distinct from the ideal debate about multicultural education as represented by the deliberations of the Rampton-Swann Commttee (Department of Education and Science 1981 and 1985).

One theme which has been noticeably missing from the agenda outlined above has been the assessment of performance of minority children which has in fact been the main theme of most public discussion of these issues. This is no accident. If in fact it can be shown that there are so many defects in the existing system of provision, so many obstacles standing in the way of equality of opportunity for the immigrant child, the fact of unequal performance would not appear as problematic. We would deal with the systems problems first and then go on to see what the effect of changes in these areas were. We would not begin with low 'West Indian' performance as an intractable problem and then go on painfully to explore its correlates in the home and community as well as in the school.

The Rampton Committee represented a formal response to all the confused issues which had been thrown up by the presence of minority children in schools. It based itself upon a confused consensus. It was supposed to be the enquiry which dealt with the problems of minority children and with multi-cultural education, but all the more general problems were subordinated to the one question which had been thrown up by the Parliamentary Select Committee, namely that of low 'West Indian' performance. A first volume was to be devoted to this special theme before the Committee got on with its more general job and the signs are that, even with this task complete the same theme will take precedence over others in the second volume.

In many ways the Rampton Committee report and the manner in which it reached its conclusions should be a central topic for research rather than as the work of a body of researchers arriving at objective and practical conclusions. It represented an attempt in a society marked by a confused amalgam of racism and idealism to reach a consensus on a practical problem. Its personnel were selected by a Labour Minister of Education and drawn from educational administrators, teachers and race relations practitioners, including a minority of Black members. Its composition and its conclusions were not, however, entirely acceptable to a Conservative Minister who was to receive its first report and the publication of that report took place in politically charged circumstances. According to an inspired leak in The Times before the publication of the report the Chairman Mr Anthony Rampton had been unable to control the Blacks and radicals on his committee and they had attributed West Indian failure to teachers racism rather than to home background. In this glossed version of the report, West Indian failure was assumed and the issue was whether the teachers or the home and community were to blame.

In fact the report, whatever its inadequacies, was more complex than the press leaks suggested. Taking a sample of English, Asian and West Indian children from a selection of schools, it showed that in terms of ethnic background Asian children were doing slightly better than English children in their attainment of O and A levels and C.S.E.'s while West Indian children were doing very much worse. There was no attempt to break down these statistics by such factors as actual country of origin, parents occupation or parents education, but the report discussed a wide variety of possible factors which might have produced these results. Both teachers' racism and home background were discussed as possible contributory factors, but these were discussed along with a variety of factors in educational administration and provision which it was thought might be improved.

In fact the report cried out for criticism not in terms of one political interpretation of the 'causes' having been given pre-eminence over another, but in terms of the inadequacy of its statistics and its purely speculative account of the causes and correlates of failure by Black children. One had only to look at the occupational breakdown of the English, Asian and West Indian populations in the 1971 census or the differing educational backgrounds of parents in the different ethnic samples to see that the results in terms of performance were to be expected, and, even if the broad conclusion about performance was accepted, there was little in the report to suggest any social scientific investigation of the weight to be attributed to various contributory factors.

This kind of debate was not held however. A new Chairman acceptable to the Minister was appointed with considerable lack of clarity as to whether he was now to turn his attention to the Asian children or whether he should produce some more substantiated evidence on the causes of Black failure (thought of now as a general problem, despite the surprising evidence about Asian performance). The radical elements on the Committee and their friends, on the other hand, argued that what was happening was that the findings of the Rampton report were being buried and that it was their duty to take their stand on the Rampton recommendations, backing their position with better evidence.

In due course the Committee of Enquiry proceeded with its work under the Chairmanship of Lord Swann who replaced Rampton. The Swann report is discussed in the next chapter.

Those who see State interventions such as the setting up of the Rampton Committee as a functionally efficient method through which a ruling class sought to achieve its objectives of subordinating minorities actually have a difficult case to prove. The work of the Committee and the way in which its conclusions were arrived at and received was all too messy for that. At most it could be said that it created conditions of such intellectual confusion that nothing to the benefit either of minority children or of the educational system was likely to occur. What it clearly did not do, however, was to make its value standpoints explicit and systematically consider the institutional arrangements within the schools which facilitated or inhibited the realisation of these values.

From the standpoint of this paper it was misleading for the Committee to have begun with the statistics of performance on an ethnic basis, but, assuming this starting point, and assuming realistically that the committee will continue to work on the problem with which it started, we may do well to ask what it would have to do in order to provide evidence which would help in promoting equality of opportunity.

The first thing to notice is that crude racial and ethnic statistics are always misleading. Clearly it should be a general rule that in all statistical matters 'third variables' should be explored and in this case the question which cries out for an answer is what it is about being 'West Indian' which leads to low performance. The mere assertion of ethnic difference shares with announcements of differential crime rates by the Metropolitan Police the possibility that those who put forward the statistics will be charged with attributing undesirable characteristics to the genes or the culture of the minority involved. Where such a conclusion is drawn it is all too easy to draw the conclusion that the best thing to do is to get rid of those involved. Obviously it is not the case that this was in the minds of the Rampton Commissioners, but in the sort of political climate which exists in Britain, its conclusions, like those of the Metropolitan Police could be used to fuel repatriation propaganda.

An exploration of third variables on the other hand would have looked at such factors as parents occupation, parents education, membership of one-parent families, housing conditions, childrens' experience of not only teachers but other White professionals, including the police, the selective processes as they actually operate in schools and other similar factors. These could not be discussed in terms of a debate about whether White racism or parental and community failure were to blame. What would be particularly worth exploring is whether White children with similar social characteristics to the 'West Indians' who did badly also failed within the system. It would at least be worth hypothesising that these social factors went far to explain what was represented as a simple ethnic difference. Insofar as such studies showed that there was a difference between West Indian, Asian and British children from carefully controlled samples, it would then be possible to focus sharply on any specifically ethnic element.

90

In such a statistical analysis both school system factors and extra-school factors would have to be sharply defined and considered. It would be wrong to exclude either from a serious sociological analysis. But, insofar as what we are talking about is a discussion of the contribution made by schools to promoting equality of opportunity, it is the school system factors which have to be given priority. After all there is little that the Department of Education can do to alter the extra-school factors. It could, it is true, draw these to the attention of other Departments but unless it does this, the suspicion must linger that their discussion, particularly when they are ill-defined in emotionally loaded ways, is simply part of a process of 'blaming the victim'.

This brings us back to the agenda for a critical evaluation of educational practice which has formed the main substance of this section. If we are to choose factors which are likely to be worth investigating as possibly playing a causal role in low performance we must have some theoretical criterion of relevance. That criterion of relevance should be the possible contribution made by a particular arrangement or lack of arrangement in schools to furthering equality of opportunity. Where such arrangements are Inadequate, Inequality of outcome is to be expected.

What we have sought to show in this chapter is the degree to which the educational system facilitates the assimilation of ethnic minority children by ensuring that they have equality of opportunity to achieve equally in a highly competitive system. In this regard their cultural distinctness presents problems, but it also presents an opportunity. The cultural values of the minority communities can be used not simply to promote difference and separation but rather as the basis on which a child is enabled to compete and yet preserve the sense of identity which gives him or her personal security. By these standards it is obvious that the ad hoc arrangements which have been evolved to deal with specific problems are far from adequate. What they have done is to solve the minimal problems of the educational system itself while allowing minority children to become defined as an underclass within that system. While it is possible to perceive the outlines of a policy which would lead to the educational system being a primary means whereby other disadvantages are overcome, what one actually sees is the reinforcement and confirmation of these differences.

IX Multi-culturalism, anti-racism, equality of opportunity and Swann

The greatest danger with regard to multi-culturalism is not whether it will be implemented in schools but what will be implemented in its name. Neither the goal of equality of opportunity nor that of anti-racism logically simply lead to multi-culturalism. In fact multi-culturalism may well be their antithesis. If we insist that minority children in schools should have something different but do not ask the question of whether that which is different is also not inferior we shall gain great support for multi-culturalism precisely from those who think that these minority children are inferior.

Nineteen years ago I took part in the U.N.E.S.C.O. experts meeting on the nature of racism and race prejudice. At that meeting some of our members wanted to put in a reference at the head of our statement to the 'right to be different'. We deliberately voted against any such inclusion because as we saw it, if it were inserted, it would be used by every oppressive regime and every apartheid government to justify racial inequality. President Botha, we felt sure, would support the Black's right to be different!

British education is not simply about the transmission of moral values and skills. It is about certificates and is about selection. Any educational policy, therefore, which prevents groups of children from getting certificates, from getting selected, is a betrayal of those children, however wholesome that which stands in the way may be in and of itself. It seems to me possible that multi-cultural education may play this role.

There is, of course, an inherent difficulty in our educational system. It is certificate-oriented, but, in the nature of the case only say 20% are going to get the worthwhile certificates. This poses the problem of what should be provided for the 80%. There are, not surprisingly, many who believe that this is the educational issue.

Those who believe in equality of opportunity and anti-racism of course believe both that minority group children should have equal opportunity and that it matters what sort of education is given to those who don't succeed in terms of certificates. Some, however, have identified the cause of multi-culturalism with

92

and solely with the education of the 80%. Thus one leading member of an education committee, when challenged to show that multi-culturalism would have a bad effect on formal educational standards, measured in terms of certificates replied 'I don't care if it does. I'm concerned with the 80% who don't get such certificates.'

Alternatively others have agreed that multi-cultural education should be confined to the low status uncertificated parts of the syllabus. It can be taught in primary schools and in the lower streams, but should not affect the certificated high-status subjects which can continue as before. Thus competition and selection are thought of as going on, undisturbed by multi-culturalism at lower levels.

In order to arrive at an understanding of how we can achieve both equality of opportunity and a multi-cultural syllabus, I think it is necessary that we should look both at the implications of equality of opportunity for minority children and at the ideal of a multi-cultural society and the ways in which it might be brought into being. I believe that if we do this we will be able to develop a concept of education which also fulfils a third ideal. It will be inherently anti-racist.

Equality of opportunity

Some time ago I developed a check list of items necessary to guarantee equality of opportunity to the minority child in school. I quote here the version of this list which I submitted in a paper to the Swann Committee (Department of Education and Science, 1985 p.238).

1. Instruction of non-English speaking children in their own language at the point of their entry into the system, not in order to segregate them permanently, but in order that they should not be prevented at an early stage from learning to learn by a situation of linguistic and cultural shock.

2. Instruction in the mother tongue so that children should not have to pay the price of not being able to communicate with their parents for any success which they may have in education.

3. The early introduction to English as a second language, with adequate arrangements to ensure that the time spent on acquiring English does not prevent progress in normal school subjects.

4. Second stage English instruction to ensure that children are given not merely minimal English, but sufficient command of the language to enable them to cope with study at whatever level they are otherwise capable of reaching.

5. The inclusion in the syllabus of subject matter relating to their own culture, so that they are not deprived of their own inheritance, and can see that it has recognition within the curriculum and within the value system of British society (this requirement not being met by paternalistic teaching at a low level, which could have the effect of denigrating rather than strengthening minority cultures).

6. The teaching of minority languages, history and culture up to the highest level and not merely in the low-status and uncertificated parts of the syllabus, so that these subjects have equality of status with, say, French language, literature and history.

7. The elimination from the syllabus in all subjects of all those elements derived from an earlier historical period in which the culture of minorities is denigrated and a positive emphasis in the syllabus on the histories and cultures of their countries as an important part of the education of all children.

8. A positive commitment on the part of the school to the elimination of racism through the syllabus as a whole, through specific teaching against racism and through school practices which treat racism as a disciplinary offence.

9. The employment of qualified school-teachers from the minority groups in all subjects and a guarantee that they will be promoted on merit.

Obviously such a programme would by itself go far to fulfilling the ideals of multi-culturalism and anti-racism as well as achieving equality of opportunity. Item 5 is the one which overlaps most with multi-culturalism. It should be noted here, however, that the bracketed qualification is all important and that it might be added that such teaching is best provided by part or full-time teachers drawn from minority groups themselves.

Item 8 covers anti-racism which is important not simply in its own right but as a means to the end of equality of opportunity.

One point which perhaps should have been made, is one which I left out because I thought it was obvious. This is that all selection processes whereby children are assigned to classes, streams or bands should be based upon academic performance and not upon teachers assessment of behaviour. I would now want to add this explicitly in the light of the findings of the Eggleston Report (Eggleston et al 1986). Perhaps I should add though that allocations to classes on grounds of behaviour might well be argued for by teachers as a sign of their multi-cultural sensitivity. This is precisely the danger of multi-culturalism to which I have drawn attention. It is on the basis of stereotypes that children are differentially treated and those stereotypes are as likely to be derogatory or patronising as not. We do best for minority children's equality of opportunity by sticking to formal academic criteria.

One objection to giving equality of opportunity the prominence which I have given it, is that such equality does not exist for other children and particularly working class children. Of this I would say that it in part rests upon a mistaken belief that what we are talking about is equality of outcome. It should be clear that we are not and that for the foreseeable future and in comprehensive systems as well as three stream systems there will be more rewards for some than for others. We can't wish such a system away and, if we believe in equal opportunity we should be concerned to ensure that all children have an equal chance of unequal rewards.

More important is the notion that working-class children do not enjoy equality of opportunity within the present system. This is true. All that I can say about it is that someone should write a check-list of items necessary to overcome the barriers that presently stand in their way. If the success of minority children in winning their rights here were to lead to working-class demands, so far as I am concerned, so much the better. The present position is that minority children are doubly disadvantaged. They are from minorities and they are usually working-class. Their minimum demand would be that they allowed the same opportunities as working-class children. For all children to have equality of opportunity, however, it would be necessary to review the system from the point of view of the minorities and of the native working-class.

The programme which I have outlined, however, may be held to fall short of what is necessary for Education for a Multi-Cultural Society. Thus many will argue that a multi-cultural education programme applies not only to the minority children and the schools where their presence is evident, but to the middle-class largely White suburban school. For that reason it will indeed be necessary to outline and give the rationale for a multi-cultural programme which includes such schools, but, before we do, it is necessary to insist that a genuine multi-cultural programme cannot and must not leave out the needs of the minority child in the minority school. Too often the notion of 'multi-cultural education for all' or 'education for a multi-cultural society' has simply left out any consideration of rendering efficient services like E2L or Mother-Tongue teaching which are at present abysmally inadequate.

Education for a multi-cultural society

The notion that Britain is a multi-cultural or multi-social society is asserted very widely and very glibly. Such glib assertions, however, mean little in practice apart from a generalised feeling of being good on the part of those who assert them. If we are serious about the notion of multi-culturalism we must specify the precise and limited sense in which we use the term.

One meaning which does not apply in the British case is the notion that somehow or other power in Britain is to be shared between the British majority and the Caribbean and Southern Asian minorities in the way in which it is shared between the Walloons and the Flemish in Belgium, or between the French and English-speaking sections of the population in Quebec. We do not expect these minorities to have equal numbers of seats in Parliament or even reserved seats in one of the Houses of Parliament. We do not expect that their language will not rank equally with English in government business or that they will have an equal share in civil service posts. Nor do we expect that they will have separate school systems. These are some of the aspects of a certain kind of plural society.

Still less do we expect or want the creation of another kind of plural society such as that which exists in its present form in South Africa in which multi-culturalism is continually asserted but the segments are thought of as having unequal power. Here again we must insist that multi-culturalism is a dangerous notion unless it is coupled with some concept of equality of opportunity or equality between plural segments.

Finally we should notice that any concept of multi-culturalism which undermines the concept of equality of treatment in the public domain is unacceptable. The right of the individual to a vote, the right to equal treatment by the police, the right to form free trades unions and to engage in collective bargaining as well as the hard-worn social rights of the Welfare State constitute a common political culture which is not only part of the British tradition but is supported by all minority groups. Any attempt to undermine this common system of rights and to replace it with a British equivalent of South Africa's Ministry of Bantu Affairs has to be opposed whether it comes in the name of pluralism or multi-culturalism or in any other guise.

But if these more grandiose concepts of multi-culturalism are rejected what remains of the concept? Just this, I think: that in a society committed to equality of opportunity in all spheres of the public domain it is recognised that there is also a private communal domain in which each community and ultimately each individual will choose his own way of life. This private domain includes the regulation of sexual and family affairs and all matters concerned with religious or moral education. Tolerance of diversity in these respects is an achievement of our civilisation as hard-won as the rights and liberties which guarantee equality of opportunity.

It is easy enough to say that such tolerance should exist; harder to acknowledge it in detail and in practice. Our society's values are individualist ones and we are likely to extend the notion of the rights of the individual to involve not merely his rights in the market place and in the public forum, but also his or her right as against the family. Thus it is not surprising that feminists find it hard to accept the limitations on the freedom of women which Asian family and marriage systems impose. Many of them would call for a radical change in these systems and in so doing would do much to undermine the distinctive communal culture of Asian minorities.

The harshness of this clash of values occurs because we in the majority community seek to impose our values without really understanding what minority values are about. In fact what the Asian minorities are seeking to assert is that there are some things which should not be treated as commodities and they are horrified at the crude marketing of sex which they see as an endemic part of our culture. Feminist values espoused by insensitive majority women appear to them only as a part of this larger package. Of course it is true that the translation of customs from sending society to the society of settlement means that those customs may be insensitively applied. But what matters is that changes in them should be brought about by members of the communities themselves. Anyone who knows and trusts Asian communities will know that members of these communities are themselves questioning and modifying their values on family matters and that it is through their solutions that they will adapt to living in British society.

The issues which I have raised here are quite central ones when we consider what is happening in our schools. Schools are in part the instruments of the larger society in the public domain. They are concerned with the transmission of skills and the broad political values of our society. They are also concerned with the process of selection whereby individuals are allocated to different destinies in life. As such they are likely to be corrosive of communal values of any kind. Yet they also assume responsibility for moral education and what we have attempted to do in this area is to foster values of neighbourliness and solidarity without which a purely individualist society would become simply a war of all against all. The sources of these values have been found in Christianity, in the experience of family and community, and in the class solidarity of working people.

Immigrant communities view our schools with some ambivalence. On the one hand they see them as having a high instrumental value. To get on in the world of the market place and the public domain one needs education and certificates. Schools are necessary because they provide these. On the other hand the school may seem to be saying 'You must abandon all your own group values when you come here and you must be assimilated' or, alternatively, 'So far as moral values are concerned you must learn the Christian and British ones which we teach'.

In response to these latter demands immigrant minority parents develop quite specific demands. They want their children to have instruction in the mother tongue and in the ways of behaving and thinking that go with the mother tongue. They want their children to continue to respect the values of their own community and they want them to preserve appropriate standards of dress, decorum, food and behaviour even if they conflict with what is on offer in the school.

At first this is a fight which has to be fought by individual families but sooner or later religious organisations appear, whether Pentecostalist Churches amongst the West Indians or mosques and temples amongst the Pakistanis and Indians and these organisations set up alternative basis to the school from which the moral training of the young can be organised. Nowhere is this more evident than in Muslim communities. In Birmingham, for example, where there are some 40 mosques, thousands of children receive instructions each evening after school in the mother tongue, in Arabic, in the Quran and in the way of life which the Quran teaches.

What are the implications of this for the schools? They are, I believe, twofold. On the one hand they must themselves provide for and they must relate themselves to the provision which is being made for the moral education of minority children. On the other hand they must ensure that all children learn tolerance of cultural diversity. The process of moral education in schools becomes a pluralist one in which all children can see their own community's values represented, even if it exists in a stronger form outside. At the same time all children should learn to respect the diverse views of others, even if their particular school happens to have, as White suburban schools often have, a monocultural population. All children should have the opportunity of learning about their own community values and all should learn something about the values of others.

A more radical view is taken by some Muslims, as it has been taken for a long time by Roman Catholics. This is that if schools have to fulfil both a selective and a morally educational function, control should not lie with the selectors but with those who stand for communal and religious values. Inevitably I think we shall see Muslim schools. It will then be for Muslim parents and teachers to ensure that the maintenance of moral cohesion is not bought at the price of abandoning material success.

One of the reasons why the case for Mulsim schools is as strong as it is, is that schools have made such a poor job of moral education and education in community and religious values. Usually taught by White British teachers, the context of such teaching is often quite inadequate involving a paternalistic caricature of the culture about which it claims to be teaching. Clearly if the schools are to do a better job they must find some way of involving community teachers in the educational process, either by appointing more minority teachers full-time or part-time or relating themselves to what goes on in supplementary schools. Merely to tell existing schools and existing staff to 'be more multi-cultural' is not enough. What we are likely to get in this way is likely to be tokenism at its worst. It can be argued that if this is all the schools can offer they would do better to leave the job to the minority communities themselves.

Yet when that is said there clearly is a problem if the perpetuation of minority cultures exists only on the margins of society. The argument for bringing it into the schools is that insofar as we are able to do this effectively then minority cultures will have a recognised place within our social system and our culture. And, if they have such a place, they should have it, not merely in schools where there are large numbers of minority children, but in all schools and for all children.

From multi-culturalism to anti-racism

It will be seen from what I have said that both the ideal of equality of opportunity and that of multi-culturalism lead to the notion of anti-racist education. Equality of opportunity leads to it because there is no way in which such equality of opportunity can be guaranteed if a group of children or their cultural background are the subject of racial abuse and if those who operate the selection process show a racial bias. Multi-culturalism leads to it because it becomes apparent that the main aim of a multi-cultural syllabus is to encourage respect for minority children and their cultures. Nonetheless it is important that the concept of anti-racism should be developed in its own right.

Anti-racism is an issue which must be posed in relation to the behaviour of teachers and pupils and as a matter of concern in the curriculum.

So far as behaviour is concerned a policy of anti-racism in schools requires an explicit statement that racial harrassment and abuse will be punished and the carrying out of appropriate punishment whenever such behaviour occurs. It also involves raising the level of awareness of racism amongst teachers, so that they take note of incidents which they may previously have regarded as usual or inevitable.

One particular and more central aspect of teachers 'racism' is the operation of a racial bias in selection processes. When students are selectively assigned to classes, bands and streams criteria for assignment should be as objective as possible. Clearly there may be some margin of discretion to allow for special cases but any case in which such discretion leads to the downgrading of a minority child should be the object of special investigation. This is perhaps the key area in schools where racial bias operates through stereotypes. Such stereotypes need to be brought into the open and criticised if equality of opportunity is to be attained and the commitment to multi-culturalism should not be used in an attempt to justify special and different treatment for minority children. Eggleston's report shows how systematically minority children have suffered in this matter, by being assigned to lower streams and classes.

So far as the curriculum is concerned there are two matters which require consideration. The first is the 'deracialisation' of the old curriculum. The second is the explicit appearance of anti-racism as part of the syllabus.

There are many who say that the emphasis here should be on an anti-racist approach of the whole syllabus. The danger, however, is that, unless the details of such an approach are made explicit, claiming to do everything will actually lead to doing nothing. What is required is the development of studies of particular syllabuses and teaching practices and a statement by Heads to their staffs that such an anti-racist goal is being set.

A commitment of this kind will clearly have greater impact if anti-racism itself is a part of the syllabus. I believe personally that this should be part of the political education which all children should receive. Generally education in politics should be so planned as to ensure that children are exposed to a variety of views. This is essential in a free society which wishes to avoid indoctrination. But these are a very small number of ideas, which should be presented as the view of all legitimate parties. Anti-racism is one of them.

One of the difficulties about developing an anti-racist policy in schools is that one cannot assume that those who will be called in to carry it out will themselves be free of racism. For this reason it is necessary that Local Education Authorities should make their position clear and then see to it that teachers undergo special professional training so that they become aware of the dangers of racism. Colleges concerned with the training of teachers must also make this issue central and explicit in training. Of course there is a problem in that Local Authorities and Colleges of Education are themselves not wholly free of racism, but the goal of anti-racism has been made explicit in the Swann report and elsewhere, and it is now possible to begin the difficult task of pulling ourselves up by our own moral and political boot-straps.

The Swann Report

We are now in a position to approach the Swann report critically. We shall have to ask how well it understands and proposes to deal with each of the problems of equality of opportunity, multi-culturalism and anti-racism. My own view of equality of opportunity as the most central concept is set out in the check-list of items given above. On multi-culturalism my view is that it is a matter for which responsibility has to be shared between the schools and the communities themselves, so far as the education of minority children is concerned; but that when it comes to the education of the White suburban child, the whole question of multi-culturalism becomes merged with that of anti-racism. Anti-racism as a policy must be seen as central to a policy of equality of opportunity and requires a quite explicit commitment on the part of all those who train or employ teachers, so that it becomes a part of the ethos of our society and part of the professionalism of education.

Swann did not start from that position and could not because its starting point was in Rampton and Rampton had been instructed to give priority in his work to the underachievement of West Indian children, even though he was also commissioned to study the whole problem of the education of ethnic minority children. The result was that the Rampton problematic which Swann inherited was that of West Indian underachievement and whether this was due to, or perhaps to be blamed on, the schools and the teachers on the one hand or the West Indian family and community on the other.

The Swann report tries to get away from this somewhat childish problematic and partially succeeds in doing so. It begins with two perceptive chapters on the nature of a multi-cultural society and on the nature of racism and only then goes on to pick up the argument about underachievement. The chapter on the multi-cultural society seems to me to be excellent and to accord entirely with my own view of a common culture in the public domain characterised by equality of opportunity and a variety of cultural forms in the private domain. This should provide an excellent basis for the discussion of multi-cultural education. The chapter on racism is also surprisingly clear and should provide the basis for the development of anti-racist policies in schools. The role of teachers stereotypes, of the climate of racism outside the school and of racist attacks and racist name calling are all well discussed and should serve to suggest specific arrangements to combat racism in schools.

Unfortunately the argument of the report as it develops in Chapter Three on Underachievement comes to hinge not on the committees concepts of multi-culturalism and anti-racism, but on its analysis of underachievement.

The argument goes like this... Low IQ is not a significant factor in West Indian underachievement. (Mercifully the research contribution of Professor Mackintosh and Dr Marcie Taylor buried that interpretation). Underachievement is associated with socio-economic status in the case of all children. West Indians do worse than other children even when class is taken into account, but what is to be expected is that they suffer an extra element of deprivation. 'A substantial part of ethnic minority underachievement, where it occurs, is....the result of social prejudice and discrimination on the part of society at large, bearing on ethnic minority homes and families and hence, indirectly, on children' (p.89). Some discrimination, however, bears directly on children within the educational system. Research evidence on this is obscure and confusing, but nonetheless:

'It will be evident that society is faced with a dual problem: eradicating the discriminatory attitudes of the White majority on the one hand and, on the other, evolving an educational system which ensures that all pupils achieve their full potential.

In the short-term, the first of these problems is a matter for the Law, the Government, Housing Authorities, Employers' Unions, the CRE and many others. But in the long-run we believe that it is a matter for the schools to bring about this change of attitudes amongst coming generations.

The second problem is specifically one for the educational system' (p.90).

What the Swann Committee calls Education for All is 'an attempt simultaneously to change attitudes amongst the White majority and to develop a pattern of education that enables all pupils to give of their best' (p.90).

In other words Multi-Cultural Education must aim at changing White attitudes and overcoming Black underachievement at the same time.

The term 'multi-cultural education' is rejected because it 'has encouraged schools and LEA's in 'all-white' areas to believe that the issues involved are of no concern to them' and the term 'education for all' chosen because it 'reflects the responsibility which we feel that those concerned with education share in paying the foundations of the kind of pluralist society which we envisaged' (p.317).

It is, I think, unfortunate that the Swann Committee adopted the rather vacuous title 'Education for All' for the programme which it presents and that it offered it as a means of overcoming the discrimination leading to underachievement. Nonetheless there is much in what they have to say about its meaning which suggests that they do keep the egalitarian and anti-racist goals emphasised here firmly in mind. Amongst the points which it emphasises are the following:

1. Education should 'help pupils to understand the world in which they live and the interdependence of individuals, group and nations'.

2. 'The richness of cultural variety in Britain should be appreciated and integrated in educational curricula at all levels'.

3. Education is seen 'as having a major role to play in countering the racism which still persists in Britain today'.

4. 'Education for All' therefore seeks 'to identify and to remove those practices and procedures which work, directly and intentionally or indirectly and unintentionally, against pupils from any ethnic group'.

5. The 'syllabus recognising the multi-ethnic character of Britain' should 'be used in all schools'.

6. 'It is also essential that the education system caters for any specific needs which (ethnic minority) children may experience in order to offer them the equality of opportunity which (has been) relocated'.

7. The concept of education for all raises immediate and obvious issues in the field of language teaching and religious education but there is a need to re-evaluate the curricula on the basis of the following criteria:

   i) the variety of social, cultural and ethnic groups and a perspective of the world should be evident in visual, stories, conversation and information.

   ii) people from social, cultural and ethnic groups should be presented as individuals with every human attribute.

   iii) Cultures should be sympathetically described in their own terms and not judged against some notion of 'ethnocentric' or 'Euro-centric' culture.

   iv) the curriculum should include accurate information on racial and cultural differences and similarities.

   v) all children should be encouraged to see the cultural diversity of our society in a positive light.

   vi) the issue of racism at both institutional and individual level should be considered openly and efforts made to counter it'.

8. Political education should be an essential part of the syllabus. It should 'open pupils minds to a full appreciation of the role which they as adults can and should play in shaping their futures'.

In learning how 'some long-established practices were originally developed to cater for a homogeneous population' of children we should also 'consider whether such practices are still appropriate to.....changed......British society today', or whether they are against the interests of minority groups.

> 'Some views and attitudes are arguably unacceptable in our democracy: racism, suppression of opinion, exploitation of the defenceless.....Education which identifies the evils we must resist, and suggests how we may resist them is quite proper and likely to command wide support'.

In principle this is a very thorough-going agenda. It is one which Swann sees as being implemented through the initiative of the DES, the Inspectorate, the LEA's, Multi-cultural Advisors, Head Teachers, Heads of Departments, Examination Boards, Colleges of Education and ordinary teachers.

It seems to me that this agenda does meet the needs to which I was trying to refer earlier. It emphasises the notion of equality of opportunity, it does not base its concept of multi-culturalism on a paternalistic and caricatured concept of minority cultures and it targets racism both indirectly through a syllabus for all which treats minority culture with respect and directly through anti-racist teaching. It certainly gives me a charter for the kind of anti-racist reform of the education system which I wish to bring about.

I would hope that all those who wish to see an anti-racist educational system will take advantage of what Swann has offered. We are no longer talking about a situation in which a few idealists fighting against the mainstream are propogating a minority doctrine. Whatever local Councillors or reactionary head teachers and others may think of the matter we have the Swann Report on our side. It is up to us to see that its principles are fully implemented. Unfortunately the Minister of the day, Sir Keith Joseph has showed no willingness to give his support to Swann or to provide the resources necessary for its implementation.

X   The 1981 urban riots in Britain

Urban sociology of recent years has been marked by its preoccupation with the problems of an affluent urban society. It sought to explain how consumption was organised, how labour was reproduced and how the whole urban system was managed in the interests of capitalism. It was in the nature of such explanations that they explained too much, because, if every aspect of urban behaviour was shown to have a systemic function, it was difficult to see in this, as in any other form of functionalist explanation, how change could occur or why it should. The study of urban social movements then appeared as something of an afterthought to explain why, despite the self-sustaining nature of urban capitalism, some dynamic was introduced into it. Really dramatic urban social movements which were not explicable as modes of incorporation or of potential conflict resolution, however, were hard to find, so that this part of urban sociology was reduced all too often to the study of any leftish social organisation.

One would have thought that the events in Paris and other cities in 1968 and the burning and looting of American cities which reached its peak in 1967 would have called for a more fundamental reconceptualisation of urban sociology, but, somehow these events were explained away as not essentially the concern of urban sociology, being rather, in the first case, the result of wide educational and political conflict, and, in the second, a unique exception due to the fact of racial conflict. The outburst of rioting in British cities in the summer months of 1981 therefore remained inexplicable in terms of most of the theories of urban sociology.

Before returning to the theoretical issues, it will be useful to recall what actually occurred. First of all, there had been an isolated riot in the St. Paul's district of Bristol in the early summer of 1980. There had, of course, been all sorts of conflict before this involving clashes between black and white gangs, between black people and racists and fascists, and between blacks and the police, but the term 'riot' had a fairly considerable justification in Bristol in that police action was violently resisted by large numbers of people, that, at one time the police actually withdrew from the area, and that there was large scale arson and looting. About a year later there was similar but larger events of the same kind in Brixton, London, one of the major areas of West Indian settlement and, unlike

103

Bristol, at the very centre of Black/White and Black/Police conflict. The Brixton riot was seen to be central to the future of British social, urban and race relations administration and a judicial commission of enquiry led by Lord Justice Scarman was appointed to investigate the matter from the point of view of law and order. The seriousness and typicality of the Brixton events were then confirmed by a renewed outburst of rioting in July 1981, followed by rioting in Southall, an area of Indian settlement in West London, in Toxteth, Liverpool, a centre of Black settlement which long predated the post-war West Indian immigration, in Moss Side, Manchester, where Whites as well as Blacks were seen to be engaged in conflict with the police and then in a dozen or more other places where young Blacks and Whites fought with the police and destroyed property. Most of these 'riots' were in Inner City areas, but there were also reports of an attack on a suburban Council estate in Leicester and one by so-called 'Mods' (a group of White youths affiliated to one of the deviant youth sub-cultures) on a holiday centre in the Lake District.

A series of events like these is encapsulated in public memory by the way it is reported in the media. Nice sociological distinctions were not made and the riots were by and large explained as being either of one piece or due to imitation (the term 'copy-cat riots' was widely used to describe the lesser events). On the margins too the press amplified the events by including under the riot heading a whole series of events which otherwise would hardly have been reported or would simply have been noted as normal crime. It is, of course, the case, that regardless of what the press said, these events were interconnected, if not in their causes, in their retrospective recollection in the public mind. Nonetheless it is important in order to obtain a deeper sociological understanding to look more closely at the separate events.

The first take-off point for the riots is to be found in the situation of the children of West Indian immigrants in British cities. The immigrant generation amongst West Indians, as amongst Asians came to Britain primarily between 1950 and 1962, before Commonwealth immigration was nearly completely stopped except for dependents, to fill gaps in the labour force left open because of the unwillingness of British workers to do what young West Indians were to call 'shit-work'. While the Asians who came were accompanied by others filling more comfortable niches in commerce, in industry and in social life, and included, even amongst those doing dirty and unpleasant work, a wide range of education, the West Indians, and especially the Jamaicans, who formed the vast majority were nearly all of about the same minimal educational standard. Canada and, to a lesser extent the United States, creamed off the better educated Jamaicans through a selective immigration policy, leaving Britain as the main target for immigration for the less qualified.

This immigrant generation presented few problems to Britain. They were reliable and even docile workers, and, though they joined trades unions and the Labour Party, were socially very conservative. Many were churchgoers, including a substantial minority who were members of the tight-knit Pentecostal sects. The Black British children of these workers, however, were very different because they faced a different set of problems. At school they did badly on the average both because, given their class background and the class bias on British education, this was to be expected, and because they faced additional problems of communicating with teachers in a language and a culture which was the product of colonialism and slavery and which degraded their self-image. On leaving school these boys and girls found themselves unwanted on the labour market. They were not wanted for the 'shit-work' done by their parents, because they were not sufficiently docile, and, in any case, they did not want it, and because, like working-class British children, they had raised their aspirations. On the other hand there is evidence that, insofar as they aspired to and had the qualifications for better jobs, they encountered even greater discrimination. At best they could hope to do well enough in times of economic prosperity, taking jobs on the margin, but as the unemployment total mounted it included young people rather than old, Blacks rather than Whites and Black Youth more than anyone else. The actual rate of unemployment is concealed by the fact that many young people and especially Black young people are kept from being classified as unemployed by being placed on Work Experience Programmes. In fact one would expect that in areas like Brixton less than one Black boy or girl in two finds his or her way into a real job.

The experience of young Black men and women, rather than youth, had already begun, by the early nineteen seventies, to produce cultural and political resistance to discrimination and oppression. Ideas of Black Consciousness and Black Power gained increasing support in a variety of more or less articulate ways, but most profoundly of all, ideas deriving from the culture and religion of Rastafarianism provided the symbolic and emotional basis for resistance amongst the most disadvantaged. West Indian youth cultures and West Indian music picked up these ideas and through reggae music there was soon hardly any West Indian boy or girl for whom the notion of 'living in Babylon' did not have some emotional resonance. The wearing of dreadlocks and Rastafarian colours became widespread amongst schoolchildren and amongst unemployed West Indian youth.

Inevitably a generation finding itself in this situation became involved in petty crime, particularly hand-bag snatching. Inevitably too there was less support than would be found amongst respectable youth either for the legitimacy of property or for those who enforced law and order. But the other side of this particular equation was that the police rarely had anything but hatred and hostility towards either the Black skins or the symbols of Black culture which they began to encounter in the Inner City. It was this which meant that Black crime was inevitably amplified as swamping methods of policing were used to counter it. To catch each criminal youth it became normal practice to interview up to fifty others who by virtue of their blackness, their cultural symbols or suspicious behaviour, were thought to be possible criminals. The situation of many Black Inner Cities long before the Bristol and Brixton riots was therefore one of something approaching warfare between police and the community.

Brixton, being one of the major centres of Black culture and politics in Britain, was, unlike Bristol already moving towards mobilisation of the Black Community. Journals like Race Today were edited from there and a long campaign had been organised there demanding adequate police investigation of a fire during a West Indian party in Deptford nearby in which a number of West Indians died. Black groups alleged arson by White racists and a failure by the police fully to investigate the circumstances. In this cause celebre the coroners investigation only served to fuel the fire. Continuously moreover the Black groups complained about police behaviour, and the Lambeth Borough Council, which was the local government authority in the area and was subject to Left control, had been demanding the accountability of the police to local government committees. A situation had been reached when any arrest of a Black youth by the police was liable to be resisted by collective action, simply because, in the view of the Black community, only direct action and self defence was likely to be effective to ensure justice.

The police force was itself subject to a number of conflicting trends. It had an active ethnic minorities policy seeking continuous consultation with the more orthodox community leaders. But its experience of collective resistance had led it to study quasi-military tactics, which drew on Northern Ireland experience. In the debate about the virtues of community policing which had been initiated by the Chief Constable of faraway Devon and Cornwall, the Brixton police had come down on the side which was opposed to the concept and saw itself, therefore, as caught in a dilemma. On the one hand it accepted the need for an active Ethnic Minorities policy, because it was in a multi-racial and multi-cultural area. On the other hand, given that it was also a high crime area it felt the need to be in a state of military preparedness and to use groups like the Special Patrol Group. Its response to issues like the training of police constables in anti-racism, the processing of complaints about police behaviour and the demand for public accountability had been minimal.

In these circumstances and with the rapid national rise in the rate of unemployment, any arrest in Brixton was liable to become a flashpoint, and, in the event, after some quite minor arrest incidents, in which the Brixton police behaved in what they regarded as their normal way, reistance occurred and quickly escalated into a situation in which there was extensive rioting and looting.

One minor theme in the official diagnosis of the rioting was the influence of politically motivated groups from outside. This was, of course, used by Conservative and police spokesmen as an excuse for not facing up to the issues discussed above. From a sociological point of view, however, the political diagnoses which were being made by radical groups in social work and politics were an element, if only a dependent one, in this situation. The alienation of educated White youth from the ideas of the establishment which had been a feature of the British situation since the nineteen sixties had been intensified by public expenditure cuts, which had affected community workers through loss of jobs and financial support, as well as their clients, for whom the situation was far more desperate. It would surely have been surprising if many of those who lived and worked in the area in voluntary and official roles had not been attracted to the ideas of the Far Left. In fact the state of mobilisation of the Black community was such that these groups were not able to assume a leadership role and they had to adjust their ideas to those of the Black groups. Nevertheless the ideological consciousness of the whole local community had been radicalised and it was not the Blacks only who were committed to resistance if not revolution. To say that those who fostered Left, as distinct from Black groups, were outsiders, was, therefore to miss the point. Brixton's political consciousness was affected both by local and national Black resistance and by national class based resistance to the policies of latter day capitalism.

Very different issues were posed in Southall, primarily a centre of Indian settlement. Relatively speaking the Indian community and Indian youth had been successful both in education and in employment. True, they suffered from racial discrimination and from the hardships which beset any immigrant community, but they had the cultural resources and were building up the economic resources to be able to cope with these difficulties. Their main problem was the problem of racist attack.

The influence of Peter Griffiths Smethwick campaign, in which Griffiths won the Smethwick seat in the general election, despite an electoral swing against his Conservative party, and, subsequently, that of Enoch Powell's speeches, had given legitimacy to a growing racist climate in mainstream politics, and, shortly after Powell's 1968 Birmingham speech, the National Front was formed as a coalition of racist and Fascist groups. The Front grew in importance and then declined during the seventies, but, as it declined electorally, took to street politics in the form of marches and demonstrations and to recruiting and mobilising support amongst unemployed and alienated White youth, particularly amongst the so-called Skinheads. Whether organised or unorganised this meant that concentrated Asian communities became prime targets of physical attack. There were numerous physical attacks upon and a number of murders of Asians in areas as far apart as Coventry, Walthamstow and Southall, temples and homes were set on fire, and, generally Asians found themselves in a situation not unlike that of the Jews in London's East End in the thirties. Provocative marches by the National Front into Asian areas served to underline the parallel.

In Southall the murder of an Asian youth at a bus-stop had produced demands by Asian youth for more militant action than their immigrant parents had been prepared to undertake in earlier years, and the local Indian Workers Association, in some ways the most politically organised immigrant organisation in the country, found itself challenged from below. Then a march organised by the National Front produced a pragmatic defensive alliance between Asian Youth and the Anti-Nazi League, a predominantly White group led by Trotskyists. In the ensuing affray a New Zealand school teacher was killed by the police and his killing and the subsequent Coroners enquiry became Southall's cause celebre.

In July 1981 attacks on the Asians in Southall were taken up by groups of young Skinheads, who used the rock concerts given by certain groups as occasions to build up feeling against the Asians. Eventually, after a concert given by a group called the Four Skins, attacks were made on Asian individuals and property, and, feeling that they were inadequately protected by the police, the Asians fought back. This brought them into violent contact with the police and attacks were made, both on the police and on property. Coming so soon after the Brixton riots, these events were seen as part of the general spread of racial and urban rioting.

There were in fact three parties to the Southall situation, namely Asian youth, the police, and White youth. The young Asians had tired of their elders failure to secure protection from the police and the majority had come to the view that self-defence through vigilante groups was essential. Still more radically, however, some young Asians argued that, not merely were the police an inadequate defence, but that they were positively the main enemy. Some White Left groups helped to foster these more radical attitudes seeking to mobilise young Asians both against the police and against capitalism as such. The alliance, however, remained as in Brixton a pragmatic one. It might be necessary to fight with the Far Left and with Blacks generally against the police, but the young Asians were primarily defending their own interests. On the other hand, it must be admitted that, as they appeared in higher education, many young Asians shared the experience of frustrated social mobility and employment opportunities of their English working class peers. They were precisely the kinds of people on whom a revolt of the Left would have to be based.

The police response to this situation was very different from that in Brixton. Faced with fighting in the streets between racists and Fascists on the one hand and Asians on the other, they saw it as their task, not so much as one of enforcing the provisions on the Race Relations Act which dealt with racial incitement, but rather of separating the two sides in the defence of Public Order. Literally millions of pounds were spent on providing cordons around National Front marchers when they were given permission to march, and whether it was true or not, the suspicion grew that they were less than assiduous in prosecuting those responsible for racist attacks.

Finally, in the Southall situation one should notice the role played by the Skinheads. The climate of opinion surrounding their behaviour was, of course, in part supportive. Every speech by Powell and other Conservatives urging repatriation schemes appeared to make the Asian presence illegitimate and seemed to justify violence against them. When 'Paki-bashing' became the pastime of East London White youth, many of the attackers quoted Enoch Powell in their support. But the existence of this permissive climate does not of itself explain the Skinhead phenomenon.

The roots of the phenomenon are to be found in the educational system. This system has long been based on class division and selection. As much in the new Comprehensive schools as in the old tri-partite system, the orientation of the schools is towards achievement and middle class occupations for the children of the middle classes and a few working class children deemed suitable for social promotion. For the rest, in ethnically homogeneous and stable working class areas, the children who are not selected get what education they can and become part of the anti-academic working class youth culture. As a strategy this works in a stable working class area. The boys and girls achieve a degree of solidarity and common interest through their support of football teams and their interest in popular music and its working class stars. In due course through their parents they obtain employment and a new adult sense of solidarity derived from a union based participation in the Labour movement.

What has been evident in recent years, however, is precisely the decline of mainstream working class culture and society. With this has come the emergence of deviant working class youth sub-cultures, some of which have a sentimental attachment to the cause of anti-racism, but some of which are strongly impregnated with racism. All are defiant both of the school's achievement culture and the culture of parents. But some themes and some groups are directed precisely against minority groups. One way of expressing these hostilities is through the use of Nazi insignia, which may be 'justified' as being, not so much Nazi, as, in their new meaning, anti-Black. Many of those in these groups suffer severely from unemployment both because of their lack of qualifications, but, additionally, because their styles of clothing and appearance lead to 'prejudice' of employers against them. They are a part of a much wider group of White unemployed many of whom direct their hostility, not against the minorities, but against the Government, the police and any other symbol of established authority.

The third major riot was in Liverpool. The main feature of this situation was that the Black youth involved were by no means immigrants, or even of what is paradoxically called the 'second immigrant generation'. Many of them were in fact Black British of long standing, their parents being descended from early African and West Indian settlers, particularly ex-seamen. They speak with completely Scouse (Liverpool) accents. Their experience, however, is a bitter one. They live in an area which is the final residual product of urban redevelopment, dreary and pockmarked with vacated sites and vandalised buildings. They suffer unemployment because they have poor education, because they are Black and, sometimes because 'they come from Liverpool 8'. The policing of the area, no doubt necessary because of vandalism as well as other criminal activities, has produced a very bad record of police community relations, so much so that the staid and respectable Chairperson of the Police Committee for Merseyside actually went on record after the riots as saying 'The people of Toxteth would have been mad if they hadn't rioted'.

Most of the Toxteth rioters were in fact Black and local community leaders are opposed to interpretations of the riots which suggest that race was not a prime factor in causing them. Nonetheless the Blacks of Liverpool were in every respect except their colour British proletarian youth, and there were White rioters who, because they live in Toxteth, shared the experiences of Black youth and not least their relations with the police. The Toxteth riots, therefore, more than those in Brixton, seemed to involve a confrontation of a sub-proletariat, willing, as a result of their experiences to confront the police.

The behaviour of the police and, particularly that of the Chief Constable of Merseyside, seemed to confirm much that had been said about past police community relations. This was the first riot in which C.S. gas, frequently used against rioting mobs in Northern Ireland, was used on the mainland. The police had little experience of its use and, it was claimed, used a form of the gas which was designed for penetrating walls against people. Later police cars were driven at crowds killing a handicapped man who was said to have no connection with the riots. Subsequent investigations of police behaviour were carried out by police from other forces who were by no means obviously objective in their attempt to understand what had gone on.

The riots in Moss Side, Manchester had something in common with those in Toxteth although this time the rioters included West Indian and British youth. In this case the Chief Constable showed some awareness of the desirability of community policing but later reacted toughly and refused to co-operate fully with a local authority enquiry into the events.

After Toxteth and Moss Side, rioting broke out in many other areas of the country. As it became more generalised, more and more white youths were seen to be participating. It seemed to be the case that there were large numbers of Black and white youth who were desperate about their employment situation, and, in a situation of spreading revolt, had little hesitation about confronting the police and attacking property.

One conclusion to be drawn from this spreading of the riots to other cities and to White youth was that what was happening was not specifically or only a revolt against racial oppression and mistreatment. Unemployment was mounting to unprecedented levels and, with the police and the government no longer enjoying universal support, rioting, arson, looting and the use of petrol bombs appeared as possible effective means of changing the power balance, of protesting at government policies and bringing about a change in police behaviour. The riots, in short, had assumed a national political significance, wider in its implications than that of race relations, even though racial conflict had been at the heart of the first events.

A word should be added here about the other experience which White urban working class youth have of the police. One important area of their lives, however political or apolitical they may be, will be as football supporters. This is the single most importnt form of social identification for many young men. It offers amongst other things freedom from normal social controls such as those which exist in school and a kind of libidinal release approaching ecstasy. But it is precisely in this sphere that they encounter the forces of law and order and it is in this sphere that the police have worked out their basic techniques for crowd control. When white working class male youths confront the police in a political situation they bring to that situation a long experience of the scant justice dispensed by the police amongst football crowds. The police, moreover, approach a political crowd with learning experience derived from dealing with so-called football hooligans.

As distinct from the Black and White unemployed working class youth, something should be said of the role played by young educated people with higher education organised in Far Left and, especially Trotskyist groups. It is easy to dismiss the role of these groups and, on their past record, it is perhaps right that their role should be dismissed. For years they have agitated and sold their newspapers wherever there was conflict and have lived in a state of revolutionary expectation. They have argued unconvincingly that each sign of trouble was a sign of the crisis of capitalism and of the need for revolutionary socialist solutions.

Nonetheless, before they are dismissed, there are several points to be noted about their role in the riots. Firstly they command greater numbers of members than ever before; secondly, they are no longer merely theorists, but have suffered directly from unemployment and restriction of educational opportunity due to public expenditure cuts; and finally, their diagnoses of the economic and political situation draws more assent from the working class rioters, Black and White, than it ever did in other situations of conflict. In the mobilisation of resistance to government policies and to the police, as enforcers of those policies, they provide an intellectual and theorising element which, however misguided, serves to increase the solidarity of the forces of resistance.

Riots represent so unusual an element in the social and political history of advanced industrial and urban societies in the twentieth century and certainly in the post-war world, that there is a danger of overrating their significance. We should note therefore that though they place a great strain on the social and political system, they hardly represent a revolution, and there may well be ways in which they can be contained.

The first point to be made about this is that, despite an initial backlash and a feeling in both the major political parties that the first need is support for the police and the maintenance of law and order, the fact that there have been riots gives a new urgency to measures of social policy which have hitherto been matters of debate or only partial implementation. Clearly riots have placed limits on the extent to which a capitalist government can pursue its policies of restructuring industry and altering the class balance of the society. Before the riots the government could assume that it had not reached the limits of hardship which it could impose on the population without resistance, and it could argue that there was broad consent to the notion of accepting that hardship. That argument is no longer possible. A government which allows riots to occur will be weakened electorally and, within its own supporting party, there is likely to be dissension about the toughness of the measures which it can adopt. This may well produce an adaptive response on the part of the state in the long run and, within the alternative ways of managing capitalism during a world recession, other ways may be found of dealing with the problems of the crisis, if not by a Conservative government, then by its Labour or Social Democratic successor. Something like this is already evident in debates at party conferences held in the wake of the riots.

At the same time it should not be assumed that the choice is simply between government by consent and revolution. There are many options open along the line of government by force. The most immediate reaction of government to the riots was to give the police greater powers and these increased powers will continue. It is now widely accepted that the problem of managing civil disorder familiar in Ireland has spread to mainland Britain, and the models of law and order now widely used in government circles are those derived from Northern Ireland. The use of C.S. gas and water cannon and the passing of a new Riot Act are measures which are being seriously canvassed and it must be expected that, if there is more rioting, such measures may well be implemented. If they are, we cannot be sure that they will not succeed and come to be regarded as routine and normal.

More interesting, however, are the measures of social policy which have been discussed. These do not involve a return to a state in which there is full employment and in which the great bulk of the population consent to government policies because they guarantee privatised family security. What they do involve much more is the management of a state of permanent unemployment. The main response in fact has been to try to discover normal institutionalised ways which involve neither employment or total unemployment, but which rather keep the young unemployed off the streets and given them a sufficiently high morale to be opposed to violence as a way of changing things. Thus the Youth Opportunities Programme, originally an emergency measure to allow unemployed youth to have work experience in offices and factories, even if they did not actually have jobs, is to be extended and apparently made a permanent feature of institutional provision. This represents a dramatic change in the structure of an industrial society, allowing for the creation of new institutions and forms of social control between education and the school system, on the one hand, and industry and employment on the other. It remains to be seen whether improved versions of these schemes may work, particularly those forms which involve training as distinct from work experience. Its first measures will simply gamble on being able to hold a large part of the young labour force in the anterooms of employment.

The second set of measures being canvassed is that which deals with the revitalisation of the Inner City economy and environment. Already, well before the riots, the government had embarked experimentally on a system of Inner City Partnerships in which local government would co-operate with central government departments, particularly those of the Environment and Trade and Industry to try to bring back employment to the Inner City itself and to improve its physical appearance. That is being done even with limited resources and the Conservative government has supplemented the policy by creating so called Free Enterprise Zones, in which capitalist investors will face fewer restrictions and get more government incentives than normal, to encourage the growth of their firms.
So far these policies have been limited by a crude environmentalist ideology. They do not spell out the ways in which the actual inhabitants of the inner city will benefit from the change and, indeed, the White Paper, Policy for the Inner Cities (Department of the Environment 1977a) actually suggested the removal from the Inner City of large parts of their existing population. What may well happen therefore will be a kind of publicly sponsored gentrification of the Inner City, even if in the British situation this means a reconquest of the Inner City and its sub-proletarian population by the stable and established sections of the working class. It need hardly be said that, if the policy works out in this way, it will do little to achieve the consent of those most affected. They will simply move to continue their resistance elsewhere, perhaps on the Council estates, or we may see riots occasioned by a policy of forced dispersal. The riots, however, may have increased awareness of these problems and attempts may be made to develop the Inner City and its educational institutions so that the Inner City population, including minority youth, do benefit. But all of this of course requires expenditure, and it is hard to see how these resources will be forthcoming in times of economic recession.

Another line of development likely will involve changes in policing practice. Some way may be found of making the police responsible to elected local authorities and not simply directly to the Home Secretary, although the increasing militancy of local authorities may well prevent a Conservative government from taking this step. More likely is the spread of community policing through which the police develop personal relations with Inner City residents on a street by street basis and actually take the initiative in improving social facilities like youth clubs and sports clubs. At the moment the police argue internally about this and the case for community policing is far from won, but the fact that some areas which had community policing did not riot, may strengthen the case for it. What we shall see therefore is likely to be the development of much more sophisticated forms of social control by the police than mere dependence on water cannon and C.S. gas.

Finally the government is likely to be motivated to improve race relations in a variety of ways. It already spends small sums through various programmes in giving aid to self help schemes in the West Indian community and will no doubt spend more since the schemes are at least effective in buying off the militancy of some leaders. Both parties may also become increasingly aware of the needs of their Black constituents as, more and more, they exercise control of Inner City constituencies. Programmes will be developed to ensure that general provision for the socially disadvantaged finds its way to Black as well as White recipients, and attempts will be made to deal with the problems of overt and institutionalised racism and racist attacks. The capacity of government to move along these lines, however, is likely to be severely limited in the immediate future because the other alternative response to minority rights in the Inner City is to demand their expulsion either from the Inner City or from the country.

All in all, what we are saying is that the urban riots represent some threat but not necessarily a totally disastrous one to the stability of urban industrial capitalism. A variety of reactions may be expected. One is to use such severe and punitive measures as actually to escalate the situation. A second is more and more to resort to force. A third would be to develop secondary institutions like Youth Employment Programmes simply to control the potential rioters and get them off the street. A fourth would be to develop much more sophisticated measures which make it possible for social control to be exercised through a measure of consent. Finally there is the possibility of the government being pushed into measures which do actually involve an expanded and planned economy with sufficient people, including young people, having a stake in it, for rioting to be unnecessary.

What then do these events, the riots and responses teach us about the sociology of urban capitalist society?

Some years ago I suggested an approach to urban sociology which seemed relevant to the problems of race relations in cities (Rex and Moore 1967). I suggested that one of the important bases of class formation in cities was access to housing of differing degrees of desirability. In these terms one could distinguish a number of 'housing classes' but the most important were those who through the credit provided by building societies could obtain ownership of desired suburban housing and those who through the exercise of political power had access to rented Council housing. The position of minorities was that they were denied access to either of these types of housing and were forced to find other means of housing themselves. Inter alia this meant the concentration of minority workers in certain types of occupancy and in certain parts of the city, so that from the point of view of class formation in the wider sense, these workers were likely to be dissociated in their organisational life from the mainstream working class. Even if it was admitted that housing was not the prime basis for class formation on the level of 'class-for-itself', therefore, I argued that on the level of conscious group affiliation and action, possibly that is, on the level of class-for-itself, the minorities formed or tended to form a separate class. I also argued that, whatever unity there was between black and white workers at the workplace, conflict was likely to occur over housing which was the prime cause of hostility by White workers against Blacks.

Some years later I thought that it would be useful to consider, not simply the housing class position of minorities, but their position in industry and in the education system. I concluded that the immigrant minorities tended to be in the less desirable parts of the labour market, to be concentrated in inferior and largely segregated housing, and to attend schools which were becoming increasingly segregated, and in which they were denied equality of opportunity. It could be argued therefore that, occupying an inferior class position in each of these spheres, they found themsleves overall in an 'underclass' position, distinguished by their inferior access to various forms of property and power (Rex and Tomlinson 1979). In saying this, I dissociated myself from the concept of 'underclass' as developed by Myrdal (1964) who thought the term to imply a mass of individuals who were essentially negatively defined, unemployed and increasingly unemployable and caught in a tangle of pathologies and a culture of poverty. I suggested that their distinction from the mainstream and incorporated working class did not mean that they dropped out in despair. Rather they formed their own 'underclass-for-itself' with its own forms of organisation, culture, political goals and ideology. At the level of subjective consciousness I suggested that this underclass-for-itself was much more solidly based in parts of the cities than it was in industry, although I recognised the relationship between their ideologies aned both industrial and Third World struggles.

Although I saw this conceptualisation as introducing into urban sociology an emphasis on class struggle which on the whole had been sadly lacking in the discipline, I was criticised, and I think rightly, for certain emphases which seemed to be in contradiction to the new Marxist urban sociology (Castells 1977) which was developing. It was suggested for instance that the issues which I was discussing properly belonged under the heading of the social reproduction of labour or under that of collective consumption, whereas a proper class analysis should be located in the sphere of production.

I would now fully accept that the causes of long term class struggle and political action lie in the sphere of industry and employment. The theory of housing classes is useful simply as a means of describing shorter term urban political conflict. What worries me, however is the extent to which my critics ignore the extent of conflict in such spheres as housing and education. What has been developed too often is a functionalist and deterministic theory of the social reproduction of labour and collective consumption. These seem to be thought of as smooth functioning parts of the capitalist system or at best minor conflicts of consumer interests. What I would suggest is that conflict and contradiction are to be found in each of these spheres and that it is the overdetermination of conflicts in the economic sphere by those on these other levels which determines the actual course of urban conflict and urban politics.

I also remain unrepentant in sticking to the problematic of class-for-itself and class-for-itself (the so-called historicist problematic rejected by Poulantzas, (1973)). It seems to me to be important for the study of political events to retain a concept of meaningful political action. Individuals and groups of individuals act. Systems do not. On this level it seems to me that the actual formation of groups and classes as political actors must take account not merely of their objective interests in the industrial and economic sphere but of their objective and subjective interest in the spheres of the reproduction of labour and collective consumption. Men and women that is, act collectively and consciously not solely in relation to their position in the productive system, but in relation to housing and educational opportunities and to the forces of law and order. In all these spheres they organise for conflict.

It is true, of course, that those who control and manage the capitalist system will develop strategies for the reproduction of labour and will allow for collective as well as individual consumption. It is also true that when the arrangements set up in these spheres are challenged or become ineffective they will pursue other alternatives within the system. But it is also the case that any of these arrangements are subject to class struggle and that ultimately it might prove impossible to make any adequate adjustment within the system.

The urban riots in Britain represent a phase in the development of class struggle on all the levels of the urban system which we have been discussing. On the one hand it may be argued that it is finally the fact of mass unemployment which provides the breaking point which leads to violence and the temporary breakdown of law and order. On the other, however, it is also the case that a whole range of different types of disadvantage has contributed to the alienation of the rioters, and that the ultimate conflict is not directly with employers, but with the police, and in the place where people live rather than where they work.

It is also the case that, however important the structural strains imposed on the system by the revolt of organised labour and the unemployed as such, the fundamental form of political class struggle, the actual structure of the riots depends upon much more finely tuned relationships between 'classes' and interest groups in a variety of institutional spheres. What has been shown here in a review of the actual historical events which occurred in Britain in 1981 is that Black West Indian youth or a goodly section of such youth found themselves in a particular situation in which they were in conflict with the police. The Asians of Southall found themselves in another situation in which they were attacked by a minority of White youth and fought against them and against the police. The Skinheads who attacked the Asians represent another group with a particular relationship to the educational system, to the police and to the Asians. The Black and White British of Liverpool again are concerned about their relationship or lack of relationship to the labour market, but also to the housing system and above all to the police. Again there are the mass of unemployed youth, Black and White in the country at large, who may well be involved in a struggle for jobs or a protest against their lack of availability. Finally there are the disaffected young educated Whites who approach their conflicts with the police and with the state with a highly developed political ideology which relates their problems to the crises of the capitalist system. The course of any class struggle must depend upon the alliances struck between all of these groups and the convergences and differences of interest between them.

What clearly has happened during 1981 in Britain is that all of these groups have come closer together at least temporarily and that they have opposed the system in which they live, its arrangements for the social reproduction of labour and collective consumption, and, in so doing, have challenged its normal institutions. What we see at the moment is the attempts by the Government and the State to produce a new set of social arrangements and a new form of social control. This new set of arrangements will be the basis of new class struggles between all of the groups mentioned and others whose interests are affected, whether these be immediately in the economic, the urban housing or the educational sphere. But, whatever classes are involved, and whatever the institutional focus of their conflicts, those conflicts are likely to be fought out on an urban terrain. If the Inner City is anything it is the site of the complex class struggles of contemporary capitalism.

XI Law and order in multi-racial inner city areas – the issues after Scarman

The events which occurred in Brixton, Southall, Toxteth and other places in the summer of 1981 posed the question as it had not been posed for a very long time of the role of the police in society. This has been largely overlooked because of widespread understanding in political quarters as to what the enquiry conducted by Lord Scarman was about (Scarman 1981). His report is commonly thought to have been a report on race relations and it is true that issues were confused by the fact that, once he had been appointed, there was a clamour for an enquiry into the so-called 'social' causes. Scarman, however, was a Judge and his true competence was limited strictly to legal and police matters. Clearly no one man without sociological training could in the time available possibly have produced a satisfactory account of the social causes and what was included in the report on these questions was pretty well the received and often dubious wisdom of the main departments concerned with race relations matters.

This interpretation of Scarman seems the more justified because of what has happened or not happened subsequently. Had the riots been due to social causes like unemployment, poor schooling and lack of social facilities they clearly would have recurred in 1982, 1983 and 1986 because in all these areas things have actually got worse since 1981. What has received more consideration is the effectiveness of policing and there have been changes there both in the direction of greater effectiveness in police control of the areas and in greater sensitivity to community responses, whether or not these changes were in accordance with Scarman's specific recommendations. Temporarily at least the police were held back from doing their job in ways which in 1981 provoked riot. Riots did recur in Brixton in 1985 after the shooting of an innocent woman during a police raid on a house. What still has to be demonstrated is that the changes initiated are sufficiently strong and permanent to produce a lasting law and order situation which is regarded as legitimate by the communities concerned.

Before we look at Scarman's findings or his recommendations we should perhaps stop and ask ourselves what exactly we expect of police in modern urban society. Are they to be thought of as a strictly non-political force whose task it is to protect life and property and at the same time to guarantee the rights of individuals to pursue political interests in a normal way? Are they, on the other hand, to be thought of as representing the interests of one section of society and using 'legitimate' physical coercion against certain other groups defined in terms of class or age or race. Or, finally, do we in fact accept to some extent that we live in a police state in which the police are not ultimately subject to political authority, and in which they, rather than the politicians decide what kind of law and order shall be enforced?

Clearly there are certain understandings which have been worked out between police, politicians and public about the limits of police intervention in industrial conflicts, in political demonstrations and, more generally, in community affairs. In industrial conflicts we think of it as the duty of the police to allow legal picketing but to intervene if either side appears to be breaking the rules of the game. Obviously this does not prevent the police from sometimes being charged with bias, but the important thing is simply that this is a recognised area of debate. Again, so far as marches and street demonstrations are concerned, our understanding is that where such activities do not have a clearly illegal aim, they should be permitted and that it is the duty of the police to facilitate them. We prefer it to be left to elected politicians to say which kinds of demonstatration are and which are not illegal and we try to limit police discretion as much as possible. Finally, in homogeneous communities, and particularly in working class communities the 'heaviness' of policing, that is the extent to which laws limiting social practices are enforced, may be limited by the degree of public consent. Thus, for example, the police may wink at violations of the law relating to drink and gambling and law and order will not break down because the community sets its own limits to what is and what is not permissible.

An alternative to this liberal model of the role of police in a democratic society is the model of their role in a class state. Such a model is of course never suggested as an ideal. Even if it were a guide to policy it would actually be disguised in terms of the liberal model. It is, however, the model which critics often use to explain actual police behaviour. The police are seen as central to the repressive state apparatuses which are concerned with maintaining the rule of the dominant class and suppressing opposition to it.

In my own view what has happened in Britain with the rise of working-class political power and the emergence of the Welfare State is that the second model has become less applicable than it once was and that the existence of such power means that the police are forced to work within the framework of the first so far as the working classes are concerned. This is something which one may expect to see for fairly long periods, though, of course, a radical move of politics to the right and the decline of working class power might well be expected to see the revival of the role of police as agents of a class state. Some would argue that the police did revert to this role during subsequent industrial disputes, particularly during the miners' strike of 1984-85. What is more important, however, from the point of view of this chapter is that, although a liberal pattern of policing may have prevailed so far as the working classes are concerned something far more akin to the repressive class state model may have operated in the policing of immigrant areas. While most White people in Britain feel that they can ultimately rely on the police to defend them, for many young Blacks they seem an alien force or an occupying army. In a word - in fact in the word most widely used today by young Blacks - they represent Babylon.

But just as our government is unlikely to admit to setting up repressive apparatuses to act against the working classes, so it will not publicly admit to setting them up against racial minorities. There may, of course, be a measure of hypocrisy about this and the more so in the case of racial minorities than in the case of the working classes, but even the mere protestation of high moral ideals

116

makes some difference to a society and the police may well find that there is little support in public discourses for overt oppression of Black people. The problem then is whether they still act illegitimately, that is to say, without public support.

In fact there is a fundamental contradiction in our society between our ideological professions and our actual practice. The result of this is the emergence of illegitimate political forces which follow through the practice without being burdened by ideological professions. More than this they may actually challenge formal ideologies and develop their own alternative ones. Thus while British governments have vacillated between high-sounding ideological professions and de facto acceptance of discrimination and oppression in racial matters, extreme right wing groups have arisen which do not hesitate and are quite open about encouraging racial attacks. As they put it, using a racist phase, they are prepared to call a spade a spade.

The question which we have to ask is how the police relate to groups of this kind. Do they allow them a place within the liberal consensus, facilitating their political activities along with those of, say, trade unions or peace demonstrators? More than this, and worse than this from a liberal point of view, do they themselves use their control of legitimate violence to further the racialist policies of the extreme right? Are the police in fact an independent racialist force in their own right?

To ask these questions is not to assert any particular answer to them. In fact aspects of police organisation and behaviour can be found which fit the liberal model, the class model and the police state model both in relation to the policing of the working classes and in relation to the policing of racial minorities. Our task in the first place must be to use these models as ideal types to interpret social reality, and we should certainly resist any attempts by the police public relations apparatus to deny us the right to ask such questions. Beyond this, however, there is a further task. Since there are those in the police as well as outside who allow their behaviour to be influenced by all three models we also have to ask which model will prevail or what kind of resultant of conflicting pressures will emerge..

There has in fact been little in the way of objective evidence on what happens in the policing of multi-racial inner city areas which would enable us to carry out either the interpretative task of seeing to what extent the different models of policing are operating or the more predictive one of suggesting what kind of resultant will emerge. On the one hand there are works like that of the journalist Derek Humphrey (1982) and the publication of the Lambeth Council before the riots in Brixton (1981), which simply document Black minority complaints without really testing their validity. On the other there are the press releases of Scotland Yard suggesting high rates for particular crimes amongst Blacks which on the whole do not stand up to critical scrutiny. More recently there has, it is true, been a more thoroughgoing study by the Policy Studies Institute (Smith 1983) which is to be published after this chapter was written, but insofar as this was a study commissioned by the Commissioner of Metropolitan Police, it may also be thought to have limitations. Despite this the study made clear the degree to which racism was endemic in the culture of police stations.

In these circumstances the Scarman Enquiry does have considerable importance. It is, of course, not of itself an objective study. Perhaps the best way to define it is to say that it both sought to discover whether proper policing procedures were operating and at the same time to say what those proper policing procedures might be. If anything its ideological stance is that of the liberal policing model though it necessarily modifies this as it spells out its meaning in a specific context. What is most important about the report, however, is that it is an attempt by government at the highest institutional level to gather and assess the evidence and reach policy conclusions. In what follows we will look at what Scarman found and the recommendations which he made.

The fact that what Scarman actually said should actually itself be almost an object of research is a result of the fact that the Enquiry and the Report came quite widely to be viewed as a study in race relations. This was due to the fact that the Labour Opposition and the liberal members of all political parties partially misunderstood what was intended when the enquiry was announced. Thinking that it would be the kind of enquiry which would apportion guilt and that the focus would be on the criminal intentions of the young Blacks, they insisted upon an enquiry into 'the social causes'. What they overlooked was that the enquiry would also be one into policing methods and that this was what Lord Scarman was particularly well equipped to do. Since, however, the demand for the social causes investigation was conceded and the task of doing it was assigned to Scarman what one has in the report is on the one hand a meticulously careful account of the events which occurred together with a set of important if arguable recommendations regarding police procedure, on the other, a set of propositions about the causes and remedies or race relations problems which were presumably put together by civil servants on the basis of reports received more or less at random which sometimes simply represent civil service wisdom and are sometimes fatuous and misleading. What we can gain from the Scarman Report however is an important insight into what happened in Brixton and into the sociology of policing as it appears to someone as eminent as Lord Scarman.

The first and surprising thing to stand out when one rereads the report in a calmer atmosphere than prevailed when it first came out relates to the actual events which triggered the riots. What is surprising is that these events strictly speaking had nothing to do either with social causes or with the commission of crime. What they did show very strikingly was that a situation existed in which actions which seemed routine and legitimate to the police were seen by the population at large to be threatening and aggressive.

The event which triggered the first phase of the rioting was, according to the police, an attempt by a policeman to rescue and give first aid to a bleeding man running from several others who had stabbed him. Strangely, there is no record of any attempt to arrest the man's attackers though that may indeed have occurred. But, even if we allow that the policeman concerned was motivated by the highest humanitarian aims and was not actually intent on arresting an injured man for being involved in an affray, what is clear is that the bystanders did not see it that way. They believed that the man concerned needed medical attention and did not believe that he would get it if this was left to the police. There was no way in which they could see that policeman as a protector and friend. Even what he was to represent as a humanitarian act was seen by the community as an attack.

The second incident was of a more routine kind. Marijuana is widely used in the West Indian community and the police use their powers to stop and search where there is reason to suspect possession of the drug. The widespread claim in the community is that they use such powers even when there is no reasonable ground for suspicion and that such stopping and searching is one of the main ways in which the community is 'harrassed'. It was not surprising then that when the police saw a taxi-driver stuffing pound notes into his socks they claimed that they thought these were packets of marijuana and decided to search him. Equally it is not surprising that the crowds watching became angry and truculent and resisted the police search.

Beyond these triggering events, of course, all sorts of other decisions were made about the appropriate police action and at each stage decisions were made which escalated the conflict. Numerous criminal acts were committed by those who had originally only been onlookers as they took part in resistance to the police and each time they were dealt with police action against them produced more resistance. Very soon stones were being thrown, cars were being set on fire and shops were being looted. From an original set of simple police actions a situation which seemed to be approaching a local uprising or civil war seemed to be in progress. The officers commanding the police began to talk of military strategies and comparisons were made with Belfast.

The police would see the account of the Brixton events in the above paragraphs, even though it is based on Scarman, as profoundly biassed against the police. Many of them believe that, given the existence of a large criminal minority amongst those on the streets, the reactions of the public were not simply those of innocent outrage. Criminal gangs were using these events to undermine law and order and behind them were various groups of political agitators waiting for any chance to foment revolution. More moderately there are some who would say that, in the event, a policeman arresting a potentially dangerous criminal, cannot be expected to act with the sort of nicety required by his liberal critics and that, faced with the need for rapid decisions on the spot, any sensible policeman would have done what was done and that in these circumstances riot was inevitable.

Such police reactions are understandable and there is no doubt an interpretation of the events which is distorted in that it assumes that the members of the public who became engaged in the disturbances were all political innocents doing nothing but going about on their lawful occasion and being meaninglessly assaulted by the police. But the police reactions also include strong veins of authoritarianism and racism and the questions which have to be asked relate to the ways in which their task of maintaining law and order can be effectively carried out without risking the danger of minor incidents escalating into riots. The point as Scarman saw it was not only to preserve law and order but how to do it without disturbing what he called 'public tranquillity'. It was with this in mind that he made his recommendations.

The first set of recommendations related to recruitment and training. Means should be found of eliminating those who are racists at the moment of recruitment, the training which all police are given should be extended to six months and should include training in understanding the cultural background of ethnic minorities. Secondly Scarman calls for much more careful monitoring and supervision of young constables, for training Inspectors and Sergeants in this supervision as part of the managerial training and for making racially prejudiced and discriminatory behaviour to be made an offence under the police Discipline Code punishable by dismissal.

Scarman does not call for the ending of hard policing methods and the use of the Special Patrol Group and their replacement by methods of so-called community policing. He thinks that the hard policing methods must be kept in reserve by the police at all times. Nevertheless he does criticise the specific decisions which were taken in Brixton such as the organisation of Operation Swamp involving massive stopping and searching of large sections of the population. He also does recommend a number of specific measures of community policing based upon the notion that the officer on the beat should know and be known by those whom he is policing.

Under the heading of consultation with the local community, Scarman first of all abstains from making police accountable to police committees of local Councils, but argues for the setting up of 'consultation'. In the case of London what is recommended is not the setting up of new police committees of the Borough Councils or of the Greater London Council but consultation with the 'community', a term which is left ambiguous as possibly meaning the elected Councils but also referring to ethnic minority liaison.

Most of the above recommendations refer to changes in policing practice. There is also a set of recommendations about changes in the law. These include a careful watch on the development of the Criminal Attempts Act which was passed in 1981 with the abolition of the 'sus' laws, the rationalisation of the law on stop and search, a system of random checks by lay visitors to police stations to witness the interrogation of suspects and the reform of the police complaints procedure to allow for an independent element in the investigation of complaints.

Finally, there is the question of the handling of riots and events which might lead to riot. Scarman does not oppose the possession by the police of such equipment as water cannon, C.S. gas and plastic bullets, but says that they should only be used in the gravest emergencies where there is real apprehension of loss of life and then only if their use is authorised by the Chief Officer of Police himself.

In trying to estimate what difference the Scarman report has made to the multi-racial inner city areas, four things are to be noted. Firstly the recommendations themselves are very moderate. Secondly they have by no means been accepted by Government or by the Police Authorities. Thirdly some kind of changes are in train, which have some relation to Scarman although they do not necessarily and literally follow from his recommendations. Fourthly, the reaction of the police as a whole has been negative and that of the Police Federation positively hostile.

Clearly the sine qua non of any change which would ensure that our system of policing the multi-racial inner city areas moved towards the liberal model is the rooting out of racism. Scarman's approach to this is to treat racism as a clearly identifiable condition in a potential recruit and racially prejudiced and discriminatory behaviour as a quite specific punishable offence. It must be said at once that this represents from a social science point of view a somewhat simplistic and dated approach to the problem. Racism is something which pertains not simply to the psychology of individuals but to the belief systems which operate in a society. In this sense it is, as the Policy Studies Institute argues, pervasive in the police. The problem is what, if anything, can be done about it.

The major development which has occurred is the adoption of a programme of what is called Human Awareness training at the Police College at Hendon. This is apparently a version of what is sometimes called Ethnic or Racial Awareness training which is widely used in the United States (White 1978) and has also been used recently by Local Authorities in Britain.

There clearly are limitations on what is likely to be achieved at Hendon, but there are also serious limitations about the method itself. The Hendon syllabus was introduced at a time when a Lecturer at the college had just been dismissed for making public the racist quality of the essays produced by Hendon cadets and it can hardly be without significance that the title 'Human Awareness' was preferred to 'Racial and Ethnic Awareness'. There does seem to have been some reason to suppose that any outright challenge to racist thinking at Hendon was being avoided.

More generally, however, the use of Racial and Ethnic Awareness training itself may be criticised. It was developed first in the United States after the Government had publicly committed itself to an overall programme of bringing

Black Americans as equals into the mainstream of American life and it therefore had some legitimacy. It was also clear to those who took the courses that they would be rewarded for accepting its aims. These things are also partly true in some local authority areas in Britain where the authority has embarked on an Equal Opportunity policy. In fact the conditions of the success of the policy are (a) that the trainee should know that he is receiving a course in what is his employers committed policy and (b) that he knows that he will be rewarded for supporting that policy. If either of these conditions are not true then the training will at best have only a superficial effect as a training in ideal ethics removed from the everyday reality of life, but, at worst will be counter-productive. Both of these things are probably still true at Hendon.

It probably is the case that the senior officers who have introduced this training programme at Hendon do genuinely wish to change racial attitudes and there is a sense in which their understanding of racism and their aim to change it are more radical than Scarman. But the problem in instituting such a system remains that of first educating the educators. Those who have had contact with Police Inspectors and have discussed race relations with them will know how difficult this is. Certainly the present generation of Inspectors not merely have archaic colonialist, racist and authoritarian attitudes, but have probably gained their promotion because they do. Toughmindedness is far more likely to lead to promotion than refined sensibility towards ethnic minorities.

It can also be argued that to set out to improve the attitudes of policemen is misguided. The likellhood is that they will include some good, some bad and some morally indifferent men. What one can do is to insist on codes of conduct as to how they should conduct themselves professionally. Not merely is this a matter of public servants not giving offence to the public, although that is important. Much more to the point in the policeman's case is the fact that if he behaves in a racialist way he cannot be professionally successful. The fact of the matter is that the Policy Studies Institute study still found in 1982 that racial abuse accompanied arrest very widely indeed. It is perfectly possible to control this if there is any will to do so, whether the police involved hold racist beliefs themselves or not.

The prevention of racial conflict in the Inner City clearly does depend upon a large scale education programme, nonetheless, and such a programme must include the police. What Scarman has done perhaps is to put the issue on the agenda and to give those few senior policemen who are converted to the cause of anti-racism a basis on which they can argue with their less enlightened colleagues. There is reason to suppose that the implementation of Section 71 of the 1976 Race Relations Act by Local Authorities has created some momentum in this direction in Local Government. The terrain is tougher in the police, but it is worth noting that a fight is being waged there too.

Probably the next most important set of proposals in the Scarman report is that which relates to accountability and community relations. On the first part of this little headway has been made. The police claim that if they were subject to Local Government we would have a political police and in operational situations they would have their hands tied behind their backs. Members of police committees on the other hand claim that a police force which is not accountable will be the most political of all. Statements by some Chief Constables recently certainly do suggest that this is true. One at least seems intent on enforcing if possible the narrow-minded morality of the so-called Moral Majority.

It is possible that some Councils might emerge in the future who would seek to direct the police for political purposes and there can really be no guarantees that they would not, any more than there can be guarantees that police who are unaccountable will not use their powers to achieve political purposes of their own. But no institutions can ever be guaranteed as perfect. It would surely be possible to envisage a situation in which a Chief Constable, while insisting on his own day-to-day operational control regularly discussed questions of policing policy with his police committee and, more than this, modified that policy in the light of discussion. What has actually emerged, however, is a situation in which the majority of Chief Constables seem to have simply asserted their independence and even the Home Secretary himself seems to lack the power and the authority to tell them what to do.

What Scarman recommended was a statutory duty to make arrangements, not for accountability but for community liaison. The former concept requires recognition of an elected authority. The latter can be achieved through a hand-picked committee. Much effort was put by the Home Secretary himself into forming a liaison committee in Brixton and, given the disastrous break-up of an earlier committee, the police have been anxious to keep this one in being. But such committees suffer from a general problem. They can seem to work very amicably and to the satisfaction of the police yet at the same time to lose their connection with the community. One may well expect in a future riot situation that the liaison committee had been persuaded to approve the forms of policing which led to the riot. Little would then have been achieved.

Community liaison will work best, in fact, if at least there is a strong representation from the elected members of the local Council as well as of a wide range of minority organisations. They will moreover need to discuss major issues of police policy even when the views of committee members are radically opposed to the police themselves. The choice is really between open argument in the committee chamber or violent confrontation in the streets.

What such committees ought to be discussing are the other recommendations of the Scarman report, in which in most cases Scarman has suggested leaving great power in the hands of the police but argues that it should be used with discretion. The task of the Community Liaison Committee could be precisely the exercise of that discretion. There are many examples of 'hard policing' where the introduction of tougher methods has not been the result of some immediate operational exigency and where the policy issue involved could have been discussed with a community liaison committee. Again, if it is true as the Policy Studies Institute report suggests that Black Youths are far more often stopped and searched than White Youths, then it would be appropriate for the Liaison Committee to ask why and, if unconvinced by the answers, to require the police to revise their policy.

Finally one should notice the importance of an independent element in the complaints procedure. Most people in Brixton remember that after the riots a raid was carried out on certain homes under the pretext of looking for bomb-making equipment which involved quite needless damage to property. The redress obtained from the subsequent enquiry carried out by the police was minimal. In cases like this clearly there is a need not merely for an independent element in the complaints procedure. What was necessary was a wholly independent investigation. The need for this was further emphasised when a West Indian woman was shot during a police raid in 1985.

Recently it has become apparent that many complainants who fail to get satisfaction under the complaints procedure may take civil court actions against the police. Some have gone directly to the courts. The police reponse to this is to say that because standards of proof are lower in the civil courts it might well be the case that even though damages may be awarded in the courts an action under the disciplinary procedures would fail. Those who make this point seek to emphasise the importance of justice to the police officer concerned. They seem to ignore the question of justice to the complainant. One might just as well say that the standards of proof required for the defence in the disciplinary procedure are too low.

In focussing on the findings of the Scarman report we have, of course, been dealing primarily with the problems of Brixton and with those of a West Indian descended community. A quite different range of problems, however, faces areas of Asian settlement like Southall, East London and parts of the West Midlands. There the complaint is not of police harrassment but rather of the failure of the police to protect the lives and property of Asian citizens when they have been attacked.

The sorts of experience which Asian citizens have had in places like Southall or Coventry recall the experiences of the Jews in the inter-war period. Houses have been daubed with racist graffiti; burning material has been pushed through letter boxes; shops and temples have been subject to arson attacks; individuals have been physically attacked and quite a number actually murdered. The failure of the police to protect the community against such attacks has led to demands for the setting up of vigilante groups amongst young Asians and to conflict between these groups and their potential attackers. There was a Home Office investigation of this topic and it was admitted that the problem existed. Nonetheless the Home Office refused to accept a recommendation of a largely Christian group that special Police Units should be set up to deal with this situation. It remains the case today that many Asians are gravely dissatisfied with the kind of protection which police offer them.

Coupled with the problem of racial attacks has been the problem of racist and Fascist marches into the immgirant areas. Although these have now abated somewhat there were a number of instances where groups known to have violently racist policies marched into immigrant areas carrying Union Jacks and apparently protected by the police. In the reverse situation where Asian marches (usually protesting against racial attacks) occurred the police responded to racial abuse by outsiders by merely separating those concerned from the march.

It was against this background that the riots in Southall occurred in the days which followed the July riots in Brixton. A group of skinheads using a pop concert as a base and a recruiting ground set out to attack Asian shops in Southall. Young Asians prepared to defend themselves and, seeing the police not as their protectors but as part of the enemy, confronted the police as well. Previously, of course, the largely white Anti-Nazi League had confronted the National Front in the area and one of their members, Blair Peach, had been killed by the police.

What happened in Southall was not studied by the Scarman tribunal which has therefore dealt with only part of the total problem. It should be remembered moreover that there is no neat distinction which can be made between the problems of the Asian and the West Indian communities. Asian youth complain of police harrassment and West Indians are subject to racial attack. The Scarman Report is therefore an incomplete report on the problems of policing inner-city minority areas. It needs to be extended to take account of the need to protect Black and Asian minority communities from attack. Liaison committees might well expect reports from the police on this matter and should be able to demand more effective protection.

In this discussion of the Scarman report and its recommendation what we have done is to assume that what is sought at present in Britain is a liberal type of policing, one, that is, which is not political in helping one group to pursue its interests at the expense of another, but which rather holds the ring so that individuals and groups in a free society have their lives and property defended and are free to live their lives in their own way. Given this goal, certain recommendations follow. Scarman may be said to have made the very minimal recommendations necessary. Those who want to see this type of society realised will want to see Scarman's recommendations implemented plus much more besides.

A quite different question, however, is the question of what is likely to happen as distinct from what anyone might want to happen. To judge this one has to look at the trends of opinion both within the police and within majority and minority communities. So far as the first of these is concerned there seems to be little ground for optimism.

The great weight of police opinion after the publication of the Scarman report was against its implementation. Almost immediately the public was told that crime rates in places like Brixton were soaring and were out of control because of the new soft policing methods which Scarman required. Statistics were published by Scotland Yard purporting to show that certain types of crime popularly referred to as mugging were largely committed by Black people and there was systematic resistance to Scarman on issues like that of making racially prejudiced behaviour a disciplinary offence. Finally, the Police Federation has continued to campaign politically against the report with some of its officers making grossly offensive and racist speeches at fringe Conservative meetings.

Certainly, if one went by majority opinion only, one would expect that the police would continue to be a law unto themselves especially on racial matters and that, if their right to go their own way were challenged by a liberal Home Secretary, they would simply defy him. And that may well be the truth of the matter. It is, however, the case that we do now have a minority of relatively senior policemen who have taken on board the Scarman recommendations and more besides. It remains to be seen whether they have the wits and the skill to outmanoeuvre the more vocal reactionary majority.

For the present it does seem that organised racism amongst the White majority in Britain is in retreat. Significantly a motion at the Conservative Party Conference of 1983 which called for an end to all immigration, voluntary repatriation aned the repeal of all race relations legislation was overwhelmingly defeated. It remains to be seen, however, whether this defeat in the public forum of the Conservative Party does not merely result in a renaissance of various extreme neo-Nazi and racist groups as well as in the encouragement of racial attacks by minorities amongst the young White unemployed.

In the cirumstances one would not expect that Black politics would move more towards moderation. Young West Indians who think about politics today are more and more concerned with the politics of resistance and it is a more important matter for them how they prepare to defend themselves on the streets against the police than how they vote or what kind of support they seek from political parties. If they relate to the British political system at all it is likely to be through the organisations of the Far Left. The stage seems set then for years of confrontation if not actually for a repetition of the riots. It may even be the case that there are those in the Black political leadershp who do not want any change in policing policy because confrontation is what they most need to advance their kinds of political cause.

Obviously these developments will be accelerated or checked by the extent to which on other levels Britain succeeds in promoting equality of opportunity and racial integration. To that extent those who set up the Scarman enquiry were right to suggest that the enquiry should be extended to take on board other questions than those of policing. But the system of policing takes on a life of its own as a political fact and the future of race relations may well be dependent upon the kind of police force which we allow to exist. Even more seriously British society as such becomes endangered, if, as a result of their pursuit of independent policies in the race area, the police become independent of political control. That is why the Scarman issues are important not merely for the blacks of Brixton but for all of us.

Bibliography

Bell, D. (1962) The End of Ideology Collier, Macmillan, London

Bernstein, B. (1971-1973-1975) Class, Codes and Control 3 Volumes, Routledge and Kegan Paul, London

Beveridge, W. (1942) Social Insurance and Allied Services Cmnd 6404 H.M.S.O. London

Beveridge, W. (1944) Full Enployment in a Free Society, Allen and Unwin, London

Bhagat, D. (1980) 'Race to the Top' The Spectator, London 23rd August 1986

Braverman, H. (1974) Labour and Monopoly Capital: The Degradation of Work in the Twentieth Century, Monthly Review Press, New York

Brown, C. (1984) Black and White Britain: The Third PSI Survey, Heinemann/Policy Studies Institute, London

Castells, M. (1977) The Urban Question, Edward Arnold, London

Castles, S. and Kosack G. (1973) Immigrant Workers and the Class Structure in Western Europe, Oxford University Pres, London

Central Advisory Council for Education (England, 1967), Children and their Primary Schools, Chairman Lady Plowden and (1968), Half our Future, Chairman Sir John Newson, London HMSO

Clegg, H. and Flanders, A. (1954) The System of Industrial Relations in Britain, Basil Blackwell, Oxford

Cockburn, C. (1977) The Local State: Management of Cities and People, Pluto Press, London

Cross, M. (1981) 'Black Youth, Unemployment and Urban Policy', in Rex, J. and Cross, M. Unemployment and Racial Conflict in the Inner City, Working Papers on Ethnic Relations, Research Unit on Ethnic Relations, University of Aston, Birmingham

Daniel, W. (1968) Racial Discrimination in England, Penguin Special, Harmondsworth

Deakin, N. (1970) Colour, Citizenship and British Society, Panther Books, London

Department of Education and Science (1981) Committee of Enquiry into the Education of Children from Ethnic Minority Groups, Interim Report: West Indian Children in Our Schools, Cmnd 8273, HMSO, London

Department of Education and Science (1985) Education for All, Report of the Committee of Enquiry into the Education of Children from Ethnic Minority Groups, Vol. II (Chairman Lord Swann), HMSO, London

Department of the Environment (1968) Old Houses into New Homes, Cmnd 3602, HMSO, London

Department of the Environment (1977a) Policy for the Inner Cities, Cmnd 6845, HMSO, London

Department of the Environment (1977b) Inner Area Studies: Liverpool, Birmingham and Lambeth, Summary of Consultants Final Reports, HMSO, London
Department of the Environment (1977c) Inner London: Policies for Dispersal and Balance, HMSO, London

Dhaya, B. (1973) 'Pakistanis in Britain: Transients or Settlers?' Race, Vol. 14, pp.246-77

Eggleston, J., Dunn, D. and Anjali, M. (1986) Education for Some: The Educational and Vocational Experiences of 14-17 year old members of minority groups, Trentham Books, London

Floud, J., Halsey, A.H. and Martin, F.M. (1956) Social Class and Educational Opportunity, Heinemann

Fried, C. (1983) Minorities: Community and Identity, Life Sciences Research Report, Dahlem Konferenzen Stringer Verlag, Berlin

Furnivall, J. (1948) Colonial Policy and Practice, Cambridge University Press, Cambridge

Heineman, B. (1972) The Politics of Powerlessness, Oxford University Press, London

Hepple, B. (1968) Race, Jobs and the Law in Britain, Allen Lane, The Penguin Press, Harmondsworth

Home Office (1965) Immigration From the Commonwealth, Cmnd 2739, HMSO, London

House of Commons, (1981) Home Affairs Sub-Committee, Session 1980-81, Racial Disadvantage, HMSO, London

Humphry, D. (1982) Police, Power and Black People, Panther Books, London

Jenkins, R. (1968) The Manufacture of Knowledge in the Institute of Race Relations, Paper presented to the British Sociological Association Race Relations Group

Karn, V. (1978) 'The Financing of Owner-Occupation and its Impact on Ethnic Minorities', New Community, Vol. 6, Nos. 1, 2, London

Lambert, J., Blackaby, B. and Parris, C. (1978) Housing Policy and the State, Allocation, Access and Control, Macmillan, London

Lambeth, Borough of, (1981) Final Report of the Working Party into Community/Police Relations in Lambeth

Lester, A. and Bindman, C. (1972) Race and Law, Penguin, Harmondsworth

Lieberson, S. (1963) Ethnic Patterns in American Cities, Free Press, New York

Lieberson, S. (1969) 'Measuring Population Diversity', American Sociological Review, 34: 850-862, New York

Little, A. and Willey, R. (1981) 'Multi-Cultural Education: The Way Forward', Schools Council, London

Lipset, S. (1969) Political Man, Heinemann, London

Marshall, T.H. (1977) Class, Citizenship and Social Development, University of Chicago Press, Chicago

Ministry of Housing and Local Government (1966) Our Older Homes - A Call for Action, HMSO, London

Montagu, A. (1972) Statement on Race, Oxford University Press, London

Mullard, C. (1985) Race, Power and Resistance, Routledge and Kegan Paul, London

Myrdal, G. (1944) An American Dilemma: The Negro Problem and Modern Democracy, Harper, New York

Myrdal, G. (1964) Challenge to Affluence, Gollancz, London

Myrdal, G. (1968) Value in Social Theory, Routledge and Kegan Paul, London

National Committee for Commonwealth Immigrants (N.C.C.I) (1967) Areas of Special Housing Need

O.P.C.S. County Monitor (1982) West Midlands Supplement, Birmingham Special Area, (EN81 CM43/5)

Park, R., Burgess, E. and Mackenzie, R. (1975) The City, University of Chicago Press, Chicago

Parkin, F. (1979) Marxism and Class Theory: A Bourgeois Critique, Tavistock, London

Peach, C. (1968) West Indian Migration to Britain: A Social Geography, Longman, London

Poulantzas, N. (1973) Political Power and Social Classes, New Left Books, London

Pryce, K. (1979) Endless Pressure: A Study of West Indian Lifestyles in Britain, Penguin, Harmondsworth

Reeves, F. (1985) British Racial Discourse, Cambridge University Press, Cambridge

Reeves, F. and Chevannes, M. (1981) 'The Underachievement of Rampton' in Multi-racial Education, Vol. 10, London

Rex, J. and Moore, R. (1967) Race, Community and Conflict, Oxford University Press, London

Rex, J. and Tomlinson, S. (1979) Colonial Immigrants in a British City, Routledge and Kegan Paul, London

Rex, J. (1973) Race, Colonialism and the City, Routledge and Kegan Paul, London

Rose, E.J. et al (1969) Colour and Citizenship, Oxford University Press, London

Scarman, (1981) The Brixton Disorders 10-12 April 1981, Report of the Scarman Tribunal (Cmnd 8427), HMSO, London. Also published by Pelican Books (1982) under the title The Scarman Report, Harmondsworth

Select Committee on Race Relations and Immigration (1969) Session 1968-69 The Problems of Coloured School Leavers, HMSO, London

Smith, D. (1983) Police and People in London, Policy Studies Institute, London

Smith, D. (1977) Racial Disadvantage in Britain, Penguin Books, Harmondsworth
Stenhouse, L. (1979) 'Problems and Effects of Teaching About Race Relations', The Social Science Teacher, Vol. 8, No. 4, Stevenage College of Further Education, Stevenage, Herts

Stone, M. (1981) The Education of Black Children in Britain: The Myth of Multicultural Education, Fontana, London

Street, H. (1962) The Street Report, Anti Discrimination Legislation, National Committee for Commonwealth Immigrants

Taueber, K.E. and Taueber, A.F. (1965) Negroes in Cities, Aldine, Chicago

Webb, S. (1889) 'The Historic Basis of Socialism' in Shaw, B. Fabian Essays in Socialism, Fabian Society, London

Weber, M. Economy and Society, 3 Vols. Edited by Roth, Guenther and Wittich, Claus, Bedminster Press, New York

White, J. (1978) White Awareness : A Handbook of Anti-racism Training, University of Oklahoma Press

Williams, J. (1979) 'Perspectives on the Multi-Cultural Curriculum', The Social Science Teacher, Vol. 8, No. 4, Stevenage College of Further Education, Stevenage, Herts

Young, K. and Connelly, N. (1981) Policy and Practice in the Multi-racial City, Policy Studies Institute

Index